The

COMPLETE HOME

ORGANIZER

The
COMPLETE HOME
ORGANIZER

MAXINE ORDESKY

WITH

JESSICA ELIN HIRSCHMAN

GROVE PRESS ■ NEW YORK

A FRIEDMAN GROUP BOOK

Space-planning concepts and text copyright © 1993 Maxine Ordesky.

Published in the United States by
Grove Press
841 Broadway
New York, New York 10003

Library of Congress Cataloging-in-Publication Data

Ordesky, Maxine.
    The complete home organizer/by Maxine Ordesky.
       p.   cm.
    "A Friedman Group book"—T.p. verso.
    Includes index.
    ISBN 0-8021-3340-1
    1.Storage in the home. I.Title. II.Title: Complete home organizer.
    TX309.O74 1993
    648'.8—dc20

                                92-36125
                                    CIP

THE COMPLETE HOME ORGANIZER
was prepared and produced by
Michael Friedman Publishing Group, Inc.
15 West 26th Street
New York, New York 10010

Editor: Kelly Matthews
Art Director: Jeff Batzli
Designer: Lori Thorn
Photography Editor: Daniella Jo Nilva

Front Cover Photographs:
Top Left: ©Balthazar Korab
Bottom Right: ©Jennifer Lévy/Maxine Ordesky, space design.
Back Cover Photograph: ©Michael Garland/Maxine Ordesky, space design

Illustrations: ©Maxine Ordesky
Jacket Design: Lori Thorn

Color separations by Bright Arts Pte. Ltd.
Printed in China by Leefung-Asco Printers Ltd.

10   9   8   7   6   5   4

DEDICATION

To my husband, Morrill, who inspired my career

and

To our sons, Mark and Joel, who grew up with it

MY SINCERE APPRECIATION GOES TO THE FOLLOWING:

All my clients, for giving me the opportunity to do what I love.

The architects, interior designers, and other professionals
who have shown confidence in my abilities.

Eli Nadel, a knowledgeable and skillful cabinetmaker,
who first produced many of my designs.

Stephanie Culp, for convincing me to specialize.

Linda London, for sharing an opportunity.

Steve Chase Associates, for expanding my horizon.

Patricia Olguin, whose drawing skills greatly enhanced this book.

Jessica Elin Hirschman, a gifted writer, who turned my words
and thoughts into interesting prose and whose dedication and
standards of excellence matched mine.

All the people at the Michael Friedman Publishing Group,
for their talents and the hard work they put into this project.

TABLE OF CONTENTS

Introduction 9

PART ONE: THE ANATOMY OF STORAGE SPACE

CHAPTER **1**   What to Store 15

CHAPTER **2**   Types of Storage 21

CHAPTER **3**   Taking Inventory 31

CHAPTER **4**   Tricks of the Trade 37

PART TWO: ORGANIZING ROOM BY ROOM

CHAPTER **1**   Kitchens, Pantries, and Dining Rooms 45

CHAPTER **2**   Living and Family Rooms 61

CHAPTER **3**   Bathrooms 69

CHAPTER **4**   Bedrooms 79

CHAPTER **5**   Closets 85

CHAPTER **6**   Laundry and Utility Rooms 115

CHAPTER **7**   Home Offices 123

CHAPTER **8**   Hallways and Landings 131

CHAPTER **9**   Basements and Attics 135

CHAPTER **10** Garages and Garden Sheds 141

PART THREE: SPECIAL SPACE-PLANNING CONSIDERATIONS

CHAPTER 1   Seasonal Storage 149

CHAPTER 2   Linens 153

CHAPTER 3   Sporting Gear 157

CHAPTER 4   Photographs 161

CHAPTER 5   Children's Art Supplies 163

CHAPTER 6   Valuables 167

CHAPTER 7   Collections 171

CHAPTER 8   Wine 175

CHAPTER 9   Sewing 179

Conclusion 183

Sources 186

Suggested Reading 189

Index 190

INTRODUCTION

Believe it or not, I never had a closet when I was a child. That's right. I hung all my clothes—belts, jackets, almost everything—on the back of my bedroom door until I was a teenager. By the time I was fourteen, I was compulsive about storage and organization. Being organized was an effective way for me to get and keep control over my life, not to mention my bedroom. After college, I worked as an executive secretary and then as a full-time housewife and mother of two before realizing that my obsession could be turned into a very successful commercial venture. As odd as the motivation may sound, the career change proved worthwhile, and now I help others enjoy what's been termed the second most satisfying feeling in the world: getting organized.

The words *getting organized* push everyone's button probably because there's such a stigma attached to being disorganized. Unfortunately, this stigma is often misassigned. We wrongly equate neatness with organization. Pointing all your shoes in the same direction may boost your neatness rating, but if your shoes are on your closet floor, so are the benefits of lining them up nice and neatly. Storing shoes on the floor hinders your ability to see and retrieve them and even to keep them uniformly arranged. If you can't see or easily access your carefully aligned shoes, you're not as organized as you may think.

Organization is being able to easily retrieve stored items—of any size or importance—when you need them. By this defini-

tion, most people are organized in at least one aspect of their life. Typically, it's relative to their livelihood. Some people are born organizers; others rely upon a growing cadre of professionals for help. As an experienced space planner and professional organizer, I know that organizing one's life and home is

more involved than rearranging furniture. There are actually three components to organization: environment, technique, and time. While each plays a significant role, environment is really the key element. I approach organizing in terms of space planning, that is, manipulating surroundings to make them more compatible with the task at hand. Reconfiguring existing or designing new space to accommodate individual needs is the first step toward being organized. Your ability to see, access, and retrieve the items you need

Opposite: Creating an elegant, efficient closet such as this makes up for my own "closetless" childhood.

Every inch of this New York client's wall that isn't taken up by a window or a door is storage. Above: Space planning complements any decor. Here, organization takes the form of an antique chest and refined nightstand.

Space planning is about efficiency not capacity, as evidenced by this functional galley kitchen with rolling salad cart. Kitchens are for congregating as much as for cooking, so good organization impacts safety, too.

when you need them directly affects your ability to efficiently accomplish a task.

This is why proper storage is so integral to organization. If you have to search frantically for something whenever you need it or, worse, have to search for everything you store regardless of how immediate your need, then your possessions own you. If you spend way too much time neatening, cleaning, or looking for things you own, then your possessions are controlling your life rather than the other way around.

Today it's easy—almost enjoyably so—to own a lot of things. We're an acquisitive society. International communications, comfortable global travel, mass marketing, special-

interest mail-order catalogs, and the venerable credit card all bring a striking new dimension to acquisition. We can purchase almost anything from almost anywhere in the world using our telephones! Modern times also bring varied life-styles. Family members each require different gadgets and gizmos to enhance their own life-styles, hobbies, and routines. Technology is obsolete before warranties expire. So we upgrade. The more we buy, the more we have to store. The more elements to store, the greater the likelihood of disorganization.

True, most people feel they can't be organized without sufficient storage space. But the storage issue is about efficiency, not capacity. Besides, you probably have more storage space than you realize. Isn't an envelope storage space? The glove compartment of your car can be used for storage. A briefcase is storage, and so is a gym bag, a drawer, an egg carton, and a refrigerator. Anything in your home, garden shed, car, or closet that holds other items is storage. The question is how well you utilize all the storage potential in your home.

This book will make you rethink conventional beliefs about storage. Once you're thinking, you'll be able to simultaneously solve many of your storage and organization problems. You'll be the one in control—of yourself and your life-style. You might also see some results you didn't expect. Not only might you improve your home's appearance,

you might also give Mother Nature a helping hand.

Overhauling your storage systems yields all sorts of benefits. Your tangible reward is a more functional, pleasant-looking home. (Who knows, you may even increase your home's resale value!) Intangible benefits include time savings, stress reduction, contributing to recycling programs, and donating clothes and broken but repairable appliances to the appropriate charities, to name only a few.

So go ahead, organize. It can be fun, especially when you accept one parameter in particular: There's no right way to get organized; if it works for you, it's right. The only wrong way to get organized is to make it complicated. This book is all about making storage and organization easy.

"Organized" does not necessarily mean sleek, minimal, and contemporary. This rustic dining/family room is space planned for cozy meals and warm gatherings. I especially like the table, which has personality and built-in storage.

THE ANATOMY OF STORAGE SPACE

WHAT TO STORE

Left: Store only what you use. This client entertains often and needs every custom-storage inch of her butler-style pantry. Above: A client's potpourri of tablecloths, candlesticks, and picnic baskets occupies a space-planned closet.

Think for a moment about everything you own and store in your home. Everything was either purchased or received as a gift, right? Apparel, food, kitchenware, memorabilia, old furniture, reading material, entertainment- and hobby-related items—the list is endless. Most of us store so many different things in our homes, it's no wonder we run out of space. Without adequate storage space—room enough to put things where they belong or to keep our possessions from cluttering up our living space—we feel disorganized. But contrary to popular belief, it's not an extra closet—or lack thereof—that causes disorganization.

There are only three main reasons why people are disorganized: It's part of their personalities, they set unrealistic goals and expectations for themselves, or their spaces are wrong for their needs. When looking at your spaces—closets, work areas, whatever—decide

what you can get rid of versus what you need. Examine those spaces with an eye toward making each area navigable. Trust me, buying a bookcase and renting costly commercial storage space aren't storage-problem panaceas. Extra volume or area won't automatically organize you unless you know how to use that new space, as well as existing space.

PLANNING TO HAVE MORE SPACE

Nine times out of ten, *organized and well-used space* translates into *enough space,* regardless of how many things you have or closets you don't have. The trick to organized and functional space is first knowing what to store and then learning how and where to put it.

I begin by advising new clients to store only particular items and to discard, donate, or recycle the others. Generally speaking, I recommend keeping those items that (1) you or your family members are currently using; (2) hold value for you or your family; (3) will definitely be usable in the foreseeable future. True enough, most people hear this and exclaim,

Above: Clutter be gone! Custom storage can make even the largest collections appear neat and organized. Right: A media cabinet built beneath a kitchen pass-through is an orderly use of low, horizontal space. Pocket doors conceal contents.

"But that's everything!" No it isn't, not if you purge and merge. In other words, get rid of anything that doesn't fit one of the above three criteria, and store the remaining items in an organized manner. Putting things away isn't the tough part about getting organized; the most difficult step is the first and most critical one: purging accumulated belongings.

The inability to "make" more space may loom over your possessions like a dark cloud. Thankfully, there's the proverbial silver lining. If you can't make more space, at least prioritize existing storage space for valuable or necessary items. If something is always in your way, for example, or annoying you because you're con-stantly moving it from shelf to shelf or closet to closet, then you probably don't have much need for that particular item, whatever it is. Don't be afraid to part with it.

CLUTTER COLLECTOR OR TERRIFIC TOSSER: WHICH ARE YOU?

Most people save everything or they save nothing. I rarely see middle ground. With today's busy life-styles and smaller homes, however, few people have the luxury of hold-ing on to things that will invariably turn into clutter. Why do savers obsessively keep things they don't use or hang on to unusable gifts? Several reasons, actually. See if you recognize any of these excuses.

■ Habit: "Oh, I've had that for so long I couldn't possibly part with it now."

■ Perfectionist: "I don't have time to reorganize everything properly right now."

■ Wishful: "I hope someday I'll be able to wear that dress again."

■ Fearful: "If I use these lace napkins and they get dirty, I won't be able to use them when I really need them."

■ Hopeful: "This Partridge Family lunchbox may be valuable someday."

■ Comfort: "So what if these shoes look worn? I'm on my feet all day and they're comfortable."

THROWING AWAY IS HARD TO DO

To separate trash from treasure, ask yourself some tough questions, and answer them honestly. For instance, "Will I ever be a size four again?" "That gadget has been broken for six months; am I going to fix it?" "Am I really going to build my own workbench?" "Will I

ever have time to read all these magazines?" Keep in mind what sharp-witted columnist Erma Bombeck once observed about her own accumulations: Will this Mrs. Butterworth syrup bottle sell for $175 at an antique fair in my lifetime?

Having said this, let me add that there's always room for things that are especially dear to you, for whatever reason, regardless of how ragged or faded they may appear. But these should be items that hold true sentimental value for you. The sidebar on this page offers some easy-to-digest tips for learning how to purge. Get your trash cans ready.

THE MERGE

Congratulations! You've climbed the first mountain, now on to the next ascent: the merge, or the Where-do-I-put-what-I'm-keeping? stage. Fortunately, scaling these heights will be easier.

In today's tough times, it's a sin to throw out anything that might benefit another. Reexamine designated throwaways keeping in

© James Brett

Many of my clients simply can't bear to part with anything; some suffer mild attacks of separation anxiety if I insist they discard something as benign as a punctured beach ball! I've learned a lot from these clients. So, here are a few suggestions for purging without pain.

1 Set a reasonable goal. Don't plan to clean out your entire house in one afternoon. Instead, choose a specific area in your home and establish a time limit. For example, plan two hours to tackle your clothing closet. Keep yourself honest—and diligent—and have a ticking alarm clock by your side. Allow no distractions either; let the answering machine do what it does best. Plan to spend the last half hour straightening up and putting things away. You might even set the alarm clock for ninety minutes to give yourself the additional thirty minutes to clean up.

2 Examine each item. Quickly reach one of four decisions: Repair it, give it away, throw it away, or put it away. Always allow room for things you love, however impractical, but be honest about it. Place anything you agonize over, which can be anything you keep in your hand longer than one or two minutes, into a separate "agonizables" pile.

3 Next, decide the fate of each agonizable article, even if you have to force yourself. If, let's say, you haven't worn a certain outfit for a year or each time you do put it on you immediately take it off because you don't like the way it looks on you, then get it out of your closet. Take all the items you're not totally ready to eliminate from your wardrobe and place them in a box. Label the box, seal it, date it, and squirrel it away. When a year passes and you haven't searched for what's stored in that box, donate the parcel—unopened—to a worthy cause.

4 Most important, finish cleaning up the clutter. Bag charity donations, and put them in your car; return other items to the area of the house where they belong. Complete this last step and you'll have that satisfying feeling you've heard me talk about. And remember, repeat this process as often as needed!

ESTABLISHMENTS THAT ACCEPT DONATIONS

- Charities (These include Goodwill, St. Vincent De Paul, and the Salvation Army, or call your local paper for a list of upcoming charity drives.)
- Local churches or synagogues
- Thrift or consignment shops
- Recycling centers
- Homeless shelters
- Foreign-aid organizations
- Disaster relief programs
- Garage sale (Hold your own or sponsor a neighborhood-wide event. Some towns organize annual citywide garage sales where residents can buy, sell, or trade.)
- Junkyards/hauling services
- Scrap-iron or metal shops

One of the virtues of good space planning is that you won't feel guilty about keeping the things you love. This family's books and personal mementos are displayed in a noble fashion on recessed bookcases within a den wall.

mind friends and family members who may want them; donate unneeded clothing and household gadgets to charities or fund-raising drives; drop off appropriate items at recycling centers; even call a local junk dealer. In some communities, these "resourceful purveyors" make house calls—arriving in trucks to haul away whatever they think they can resell or otherwise utilize.

I know some women who trade baby clothes. As one child outgrows a size, the mother gives those garments to a friend whose child will wear that size. She in turn gives the hand-me-downs, plus additional clothing from her child's wardrobe, to the next mother. And so the cycle repeats. Often the originator receives a closetful of stylish apparel just in time for baby number two. In addition, she didn't waste valuable drawer space storing the clothes for a younger sibling. See the sidebar on the opposite page for ideas where to donate giveaways.

A PLACE FOR EVERYTHING...

Finding a place for everything you're keeping is challenging but not insurmountable. Everything you own belongs in either active or inactive storage. How the item will be used determines its most appropriate resting place.

Keep items you use or wear every day in active (a.k.a. usable) storage. Also store anything you'll need or wear at least once a month in active storage; this should include such items as linens, useful tools or utensils, work-related items, household-finance ledgers, or sporting equipment you use routinely. If you often travel on short notice, keep your suitcases and a packed toilet kit within easy reach.

Conversely, resign items that are needed less frequently, such as seasonal sports and lawn equipment or holiday china, to inactive storage. Anything that you use or wear once a year at the most belongs in inactive storage. If you know you take only a few trips a year, keep your luggage where you can reach it but not where it will prevent you from retrieving more frequently used belongings. Inactive storage is not synonymous with deep-freeze storage. In other words, don't stash away that silver caviar server just because you might want it someday, even though it's never been out of its original gift box. Purge it; don't waste valuable storage space.

Courtesy Lillian Vernon

ACTIVE

■ Drawers and shelves that are within arm's reach or at eye level
■ Countertops
■ Hooks on doors
■ Center of cabinet shelves and closet poles

INACTIVE

■ Drawers or shelves that are beyond arm's reach or above eye level
■ Floor-level drawers (in a child's room this is *active* storage)
■ Sealed boxes, unused trunks, or suitcases
■ Blind sides of cabinet shelves and closet poles
■ Loft in garage, attic, or cellar

© Michael Garland/Maxine Ordesky, space design

Above left: Accordion-style memorabilia files organize postcards and love letters too precious to toss. Left: Sometimes, what you store is storage. This client's luggage and instrument cases slide away on high closet shelves.

TYPES OF STORAGE

Left: The right type—or combination of types—of storage can add space and style to any room, even a corner beside a door.

Right: The best storage for this client's shoes was several adjustable shelves efficiently placed close together.

If you want to stay organized, selecting the right kind of storage unit or system is as important as maintaining it. The most efficient type of storage maximizes your options without minimizing available space. There are indeed many types of storage systems, mainly because we have such a variety of belongings!

Most people prefer the type of storage that best accommodates either their life-style or their existing decor and architecture. Budget, too, is a predominant factor; very often several types are combined. The most common types of storage systems are open or closed, contemporary or traditional, freestanding or built-in, fixed or adjustable, pull-out or stationary, retail or custom, custom-manufactured, modular, and item-specific.

CHOOSING STORAGE

How you want to arrange and retrieve stored items determines the most appropriate type of storage system for your things—and there are many different kinds. Explaining the varieties of storage systems is like talking about fruit; they all belong to the same food group but differ in

© Michael Garland/Maxine Ordesky, space design

salient characteristics. Comparing storage systems, however, is actually juicier than comparing apples and oranges. The distinctions are so varied that it's rather like comparing litchi nuts, watermelons, grapes, peaches, and a sundry of other fruits. The following glossary will help elucidate these differences and similarities.

ADJUSTABLE. The flexibility of an adjustable storage system, one whose storage surfaces can be easily rearranged or reconfigured, is a very attractive feature. One kind of adjustable

Above: Built-in storage can be space-specific, as this whimsical cabinet demonstrates. Above right: An attractive TV cabinet typifies freestanding storage. It also has open shelves for display and substantial closed storage.

storage system or another can solve almost any space-planning problem. Look carefully for quality hardware, sturdy construction, and durable materials. If shabbily built, some adjustable systems can be unsteady. Check, too, that the hardware is concealed to your satisfaction so as not to detract from the unit's overall appearance. Adjustable storage units can be store-bought or custom made, depending upon your needs and pocketbook.

BUILT-IN. Most of us picture built-in storage as the shelves next to the fireplace or the bookcases in the den. Aesthetically, built-ins add personality and architectural charm to a room. Functionally, they represent an opportunity to gain custom and maximum storage space. Built-in storage units are more stable than

their counterparts—freestanding systems— which aren't anchored to a supporting wall.

I advocate built-ins whenever possible. They're the epitome of space planning. Because they are custom designed, built-ins can provide storage in those awkward places where a retail storage unit simply won't fit. The disadvantages of built-ins are that they are permanent and can be more expensive than freestanding.

CLOSED. In contrast to open storage, closed systems conceal stowed items, usually behind solid cabinets, doors, or drawers. These systems, while protecting items from view, roving hands, and dust, do limit retrievability. Closed storage can also be costly due to the additional building materials. But you're buying good looks, protected storage, and neat appearance.

CONTEMPORARY. I know what you're thinking. This is a stylistic description, not a functional one. True, but not entirely. Contemporary systems, because of their sleek appearance and lack of space-consuming decorative elements (stiles, trim ornaments), allow you to more fully utilize every inch of their available space.

CUSTOM DESIGNED AND FABRICATED. Like a handmade suit tailored to your proportions, custom-designed and custom-built storage systems are tailored to your space and possessions. And like a well-made suit, you pay for the custom fit. But you get what you pay for: maximum space utilization, nicer materials, better craftsmanship, and attention to details. It's the ultimate way to get the storage you need. I could wax rhapsodic about custom storage!

Given the benefits and pleasures of custom storage, it's hard to think of a significant disadvantage, but there are, however, two caveats that merit attention. First, when buying custom units, you won't be able to see the actual final product except in drawings. You must rely on the designer and craftsperson to capture your ideal of an attractive, functional unit. Second, you can't return custom-made units. A thorough space planner or designer should show you a rendering and the construction plans for your storage system as well as sample materials prior to fabrication.

Courtesy Crystal Cabinet Works, Inc.

CUSTOM MANUFACTURED. I only recently encountered this type of storage when a client's storage requirements screamed custom but her budget shouted ready-made. Selecting custom-manufactured storage is like dining in a Chinese restaurant—you get to choose one from column A and one from column B. You choose specific elements from a manufacturer's many offerings and an installer assembles them to fit the space. The units themselves are interchangeable; you buy what most closely fits the allotted space. Custom-manufactured storage systems, typically kitchen cabinets and wall units, check in at a satisfying price without compromising personal style or storage.

FIXED. Fixed storage systems are similar to fixed-rate loans; nothing goes up or down, it just stays the same. Fixed storage systems don't have pull-out shelves, tip-out bins, or sliding palettes. Nothing moves. Consequently, fixed units limit your flexibility and visibility with respect to the space and, over time, may not meet your changing storage needs because they can't be adjusted, reconfigured, or rearranged.

Their value is that they typically hold heavier, more substantial items than do adjustable shelves. Another bonus: Fixed storage systems can be more aesthetically pleasing because there's no hardware or adjustable mechanisms

© Michael Garland/Maxine Ordesky, space design

TYPES OF STORAGE

The following is a limited list of how typical household items can be stored.

OPEN SYSTEMS
- Books
- CDs, tapes, videos
- Shoes
- Sun hats, visors, sport caps
- Handbags
- Belts
- Ties
- Folded garments

CLOSED SYSTEMS
- Medications
- Dishes, silver
- Valuables
- Cleaning supplies
- Groceries
- Underwear, personal garments
- Cosmetics
- Jewelry

PULL-OUTS
- Medications
- Silverware
- Shoes
- Valuables, jewelry
- Groceries
- Cosmetics
- CDs, tapes, videos
- Ties, belts, folded garments

Please note: Some items can be stored in any of these systems, depending upon available space, personal preferences, and life-style.

Custom-designed and fabricated storage is a favorite of mine. Left: A client's closet bureau was sized to maximize the wall space below windows. Above left: Kitchen cabinetry stylishly converts a counter into closed storage with roll-down doors.

FREESTANDING
STORAGE SYSTEMS

- Coffee or end tables closed in below with cabinets and/or drawers
- Commercial display racks
- Folding storage crates
- Industrial shelves
- Knockdown furniture
- Literature/reading-material organizers
- Man's valet
- Portable closets with cedar linings
- Clothing lockers for mudrooms
- Rolling butcher block or microwave tables for kitchen
- Wall units
- Modular wall and furniture systems

to detract from the unit's overall appearance. Don't hesitate to mix and match fixed and adjustable storage as necessary. For instance, a tall bookcase with adjustable shelves needs stabilizing, but a fixed top and base are all that's required. And if you want to build lighting into a wall or bedside unit, all you need is a fixed shelf to conceal the fixture and the wiring.

FREESTANDING. When I talk about these storage systems, I picture bookcases, wall units, tables, desks, and so on that are not perma-

Above and right: Rolling, collapsible, and freestanding storage meet in a chrome diner-style rack. Far right: Client's music drawer with pull-out trays epitomizes item-specific storage.

nently built into a wall. They stand, as the name suggests, independently, which means they're mobile and can move from corner to corner or house to house. (Tall units may be anchored to the wall for safety and stability.) Freestanding storage units can be purchased at furniture stores or through mail-order catalogs or they can be custom designed by space planners or architects.

Their biggest disadvantage is that you're locked into a particular size and shape. Finally, freestanding storage systems generally offer less adjustability and greater instability when compared to sturdy, well-anchored built-in cabinets or storage units.

ITEM-SPECIFIC. Containers or storage units designed specifically to hold certain items are very helpful in keeping your space organized. You can buy item-specific storage or have it custom-fabricated. It may be freestanding or stationary, fixed or adjustable. The distinguishing factor is that it's designed to meet one and only one storage need for such items as cosmetics, stationery, pencils, lingerie, or silverware. You can use these units creatively, however, to store things other than what was originally intended. For instance, units with small pull-out drawers originally made to organize nuts and bolts can double as jewelry boxes. Classy acrylic models marketed for this purpose are widely available.

MODULAR. Storage units that can work equally well as an ensemble or by themselves are classified as modular. A litmus test

Courtesy Techline Furniture System by Marshall Erdman & Associates

ITEM-SPECIFIC STORAGE GOES INCOGNITO

With imagination, almost any item-specific storage unit can be modified to effectively hold alternative items. Think unconventionally. Here are some ideas.

■ Tie racks can be used for ribbons, scarves, or necklaces.

■ Shoe pockets will hold lingerie, gloves, or scarves.

■ On-door shoe racks with U-shaped spokes will keep jewelry, scarves, or hats hanging neatly.

■ Belt racks can be used as hooks for robes, necklaces, or ties.

■ Egg cartons will hold earrings, cuff links, small hair accessories, office supplies.

■ Turntables also hold medications, spices, or small items in the refrigerator.

■ Hat hooks can hold shoulder bags or clothing.

■ Drawer dividers will function as belt or jewelry cubbies.

■ Desk-drawer organizers can hold jewelry, cosmetics, or hair accessories.

Custom-manufactured storage systems are available through retail outlets and can be configured to fit any space or combination of storage needs. The best designs are flexible and adjustable, such as this desk and wall unit.

for modular furniture is whether or not you can walk into the showroom and walk out with what you need, all nicely packed in a box. The most common types are comprised of individual sections of shelves (with or without doors) and drawers. The sections will vary in length, height, and even depth to allow for the greatest flexibility. A popular example of modular storage is a wall unit that includes bookshelves, display sections,

drawers, and countertops. Modular furniture generally requires some home assembly—a minus—but you'll save money and the finished product can be broken down and transported to a different space or a new home—a plus.

So what's not to like about modular storage? For one thing, it isn't always all it could be. Since modular furniture is produced for volume sales, it's designed and constructed to sell within a particular price range. Consequently, the units do not always feature as many shelves or drawers as their dimensions could potentially accommodate. Additionally, modular units rarely boast quite the same look and feel as custom pieces.

OPEN. The moniker says it all. Open storage systems reveal their contents. A basic bookcase is open storage. The most obvious benefit of an open system is visibility and accessibility. Another plus is that they're often less expensive to buy or build than closed systems, because they don't feature drawers, doors, or costly hardware.

The drawbacks, however, are that items kept in an open storage system are exposed to ultraviolet light, dirt, curious eyes, and investigating hands. Your possessions receive no privacy, and unless kept tidy and clean, open storage can look cluttered.

PULL-OUT. Drawers, sliding palettes, roll-out cabinets, and trays and shelves that pull out, lift up, and even pop up classify as pull-out storage systems. I think of them as "access

storage units." It's often difficult to see or reach things stored at the back of deep shelves, especially if the shelves are permanent and under a counter. Drawers, trays, shelves, or sliding palettes that pull out to boldly display their contents improve both visibility and retrievability. You can buy or build cabinets featuring pull-out storage. The drawback is that both are more expensive than comparable units with stationary shelving. I believe, however, that it's money well spent, and I specify pull-outs whenever possible. It's much easier to stay organized when you can see and reach everything you need. Granted, the hardware can rob you of a few inches of side-to-side storage, but the loss is more than offset by the gained front-to-back usage. In fact, using bottom-mount hardware will alleviate this problem altogether. Additionally, you can position pull-outs close together vertically, thus better utilizing the available top-to-bottom storage space. Note, however, that pull-outs are not good for storing fragile items, unless care is taken to prevent them from falling off the tray or shelf when it moves.

Below (from left): I love it! This handsome under-counter serving cart pulls out and rolls effortlessly to other rooms during tea time. Place mats and napkins can be properly stored and clearly displayed in this client's pull-out trays. Bookcase-style pantry storage epitomizes custom storage. Similar custom-manufactured units are just as functional.

Courtesy Wood Mode

© Michael Garland/Maxine Ordesky, space design

© Robert Orr & Associates (formerly Orr & Taylor)

© James Brett

Courtesy Heller

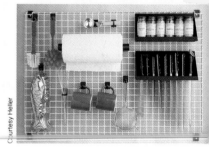

FINDING ITEM-SPECIFIC STORAGE

Sometimes the best way to store certain things—hats, belts, pots, spices, to name a few—is to take a cue from retailers. Many items manufactured for commercial displays are ideal for residential storage applications. The following are just a few examples.

- Plexiglas cubes can be used to store handbags, hosiery, or folded garments.
- Tie displays hold ties, belts, scarves, necklaces, or hats.
- Slat wall or grid wall (pictured below) accommodates a wide variety of hooks, trays, boxes, and other storage accessories.

- Eyeglass display trays can help keep pocket and purse contents neatly organized at your "staging area" to help you get out of the house quickly and smoothly.

Please note: See the sources section at the back of the book for additional information on the above items.

STATIONARY. These types of storage systems walk a fine line between fixed and pull-out storage. Stationary shelves don't slide, but the shelves themselves can be repositioned within the storage unit. If you're watching your storage inches, stationary shelves yield more side-to-side space than pull-outs because they require no hardware. I like this type of storage for shallow shelves intended to hold heavy books or fragile items. If you install deep stationary shelves, you'll appreciate the luxury of pull-outs whenever you get down on your knees or stretch on your tiptoes to reach an item from the back of the shelf.

Left: Built-in shelves, such as the ones shown in this dividing-wall bookcase, are sturdier than freestanding shelves. Two heights of closed storage and sizable display space comprise the built-in opposite the couch.

Courtesy Lillian Vernon

Courtesy Lillian Vernon

Courtesy Crystal Cabinet Works, Inc.

Courtesy Williams-Sonoma

Retail storage items such as these leave lots to the imagination. Although what you see is what you get, almost all retail systems can be used to store a variety of items or to retrofit any number of existing spaces.

RETAIL. For the most part, retail storage units are those pieces that are mass-produced and available in home-furnishings stores, in storage specialty shops, or through mail-order catalogs. The most important point to stress about this type of storage is that you know exactly what you're getting when you buy it. The drawback is you get exactly what you buy. In other words, you must make the storage piece you buy work for your space and your possessions. But the compromise may be worthwhile, considering retail storage systems are generally less costly than comparable custom-designed and fabricated systems.

TRADITIONAL. Unfortunately, the beauty of traditional storage systems—antique armoires, Louis XIV desks, or early-American bookcases, for example—is only skin deep with respect to potential storage. When storing things in traditionally styled pieces, you often lose valuable inches to the decorative stiles, reveals, and trims that adorn these furnishings.

TURNING TRADITIONAL BEAUTY INTO CONTEMPORARY EFFICIENCY

Reality and fantasy often clash; what you find aesthetically pleasing about a particular storage system—an armoire, for example—may be the very thing that limits its functionality. When this happens, I rely on a little creative license.

To make a traditional storage unit as efficient as a contemporary one, I design units that have good looks that are only skin deep and therefore do not intrude into the component's interior storage space. Placing decorative stiles on doors or drawer fronts rather than on a cabinet stile or reveal can increase available storage space and still effect a traditional look.

© Christopher Bain

Teaching an old cabinet new tricks worked wonders for one family's audio-cassette collection. A substantial "recycled" library card catalog works equally well as a coffee table and a game-playing surface.

CHAPTER THREE

TAKING INVENTORY

Whether you have many (left), some (above), or a just few (right) things to store, it's important to know the size, shape, and number. With an accurate inventory, innovative space planning can accommodate every type of storage need.

Successful problem solving starts with accurate and realistic evaluation. Certainly, reaching a workable solution to any challenge requires a thorough understanding of the problem and any conceivable limitations. The same holds true with respect to organization and storage. In order to develop a workable solution to your storage problems, you need to review existing storage space and—most important—evaluate actual space requirements. In short, take inventory of everything you're going to store. You have to determine how much space your possessions need to be properly and accessibly stored.

Counting, measuring, and examining every whatchamacallit is a tedious task at best. I've developed checklists and diagrams to help make this chore easier. Samples of these appear in the chapters on men's and women's closets. The following advice, however, deals specifically with inventorying kitchen items, but these tips for taking inventory can be applied to any room in the house that's in need of organization.

1 Look at the contents of each cabinet, one section at a time, noting how many items require special storage. Large stockpots, odd-shaped serving dishes, knives, utensils, and children's food may each warrant special storage space. Now's the time to give things away, return borrowed items to their rightful owners, and repair or toss broken items.

2 By category, count and measure each item. For example, if you stack your dishes, measure the height and diameter of each stack and count the number of plates per stack. Same with pots, pans, and lids. Measure the width, length, and depth of trays

Courtesy Crystal Cabinet Works, Inc.

Above right: In search of more space? Surround a doorway with custom cabinets and simultaneously build a charming passageway. Right: Make the most of the space you have. If cabinets are full, store mugs in a partitioned drawer.

and similar pieces. Remember, in this step your goal is to know exactly what your space requirements are for every category of items stored in the kitchen.

3 Identify and retrieve lost storage space. Look closely at how you currently shelve kitchen equipment. Measure the actual heights of the products and the heights between shelves. Now that you know exactly how much space and height each item or group of items requires, you can economically rearrange your cabinets either by yourself if they're adjustable or with a carpenter's help.

Once you've figured out the space your belongings require and evaluated your existing storage capacity, you'll know how much additional space you'll need. Don't get discouraged if the numbers seem ridiculously far apart. There are plenty of areas in your home that can be used as storage. You just have to know where to look!

THE GREAT SPACE HUNT

You'd be surprised where you can find valuable storage space in your house. As I said before, anything can be storage: a wallet, an envelope, a refrigerator. But did you know that your home's framework holds storage potential? For example, take a look behind the doors. If the distance between the wall and the door casing measures six to eight inches (15.2 to 20.3cm), you've got enough room for narrow shelves.

You may be staring at found space every day and not realize it. Here are some examples.

1 Between shelves. If you have a decent amount of space between the items placed on a shelf and the shelf above them, attach an under-shelf wire basket (sold through catalogs and at stores) to that upper shelf. You'll gain a significant amount of storage without compromising the accessibility of other stored items. Other retail items such as shelf risers also work well. Or you could build a full-depth or half-shelf in between two existing shelves to utilize the extra height.

2 Between and under windows. If the width of the wall between two windows or a window and a corner is wide enough, say thirty inches (76.2cm), build a bookcase with nine- or ten-inch (22.8 or 25.4cm) -deep shelves. After all, most books can rest on six or nine inches (15.2 or 22.8cm) of shelf space. You lose only inches (or centimeters) of floor

HOW DO YOUR WALLS GROW?

Spotting potential storage space is both a creative and a mechanical process. Identifying *unused* space as *wasted* space requires imagination and creativity. The next step, determining the depth, width, and height of a storage system to fit the space, is the mechanical part. The possessions you plan to keep in your new-found storage space is only one criterion. How the storage will impact the room is equally as important.

In most cases, if you're concerned that the new storage will intrude into the space, then buy or build something that is shallow (front-to-back), shorter than the width of the empty wall it will occupy, and no higher than an average counter or even lower if the situation calls for it. For example, window seats are typically only fifteen to eighteen inches (38.1 to 45.7cm) high. Slightly higher but also unintrusive are low storage units measuring only twenty-two to twenty-seven inches (55.8 to 68.5cm) high.

If you can't visualize the new storage in your room, simulate the dimensions to get a sense of how it will affect the room. Use pillows, boxes, lightweight furniture, or even newspapers to outline the dimensions of the new storage piece. Keep your "mock-up" storage system in place for a few days and see how you adjust to it. Eventually you'll know whether or not the proposed unit will comfortably fit there.

This rolling ladder turns taller-than-usual bookcases into functional, accessible architecture. The contemporary table design works as a mini-reading room without blocking books.

Courtesy Robern

Courtesy Robern

build out a floor-to-ceiling wall closet. Double- or triple-hang it and you've got a great deal of closet space for the price of very little floor space.

4 Bathrooms. If a standard-depth (twenty-four inches [60.9cm] front to back) double pullman eats up too much space, design a font-style vanity, which won't limit maneuverability in a narrow space. You can also gain or recoup storage with decorative wall-mounted shelving.

5 Kitchen counters. Conversely, make your kitchen countertops a few inches (or centimeters) deeper and substitute back shelves for a purely decorative backsplash. The space on the back wall between the top of a counter and the bottom of an overhead cabinet is ideal for shallow shelving.

6 Kitchen corners and crevices. This is where to install appliance garages, under-cabinet storage with retracting doors, or custom-built shelves for extra space. Also, avoid "gaposis" by looking for potential storage space in otherwise useless, dirt-trapping gaps between large appliances, between appliances and walls, and where wall space is needed for proper door clearance. Here you can install a pull-out or roll-out cabinet, an open-front cab-

space and gain considerably more volume. Most important, you have handy, organized book storage.

3 Walls and corners. Don't waste good wall space. If you think just one more closet would make you happy and you have a wall measuring four feet (1.2m) or longer, then

Courtesy KraftMaid

© Bill Rothschild/Charlotte Moss, interior design

inet for vertical tray storage, a closed, full-height-but-narrow broom closet, or a pantry. Of course, islands and peninsulas make great storage areas in kitchens and closets (for details, see Part II, Chapters 1 and 4).

⑦ Children's closets and rooms. The rule here is to look down. In an adult's closet, you would look up for unused space, but in a child's closet, things must be within reach. Because kids' clothes are much smaller than the standard closet depth, poles can be mounted at the front of a child's closet and removable storage shelves installed behind. Arrange poles to double- or triple-hang things. Freestanding coat racks encourage prompt cleanup, and they give your child a

convenient place to put everyday garments. Also, trunks, chests, baskets, bins, and tubs help keep both itty-bitty pieces and bulky, awkward things found scattered around a child's room neatly contained.

⑧ Stairwells. Storing items beneath a stairway isn't a new idea, but doing so creatively is. Rather than making the space one large disorganized storage area that's hard to stand up in, build shelves and hang hooks. Make the area a coat closet, a home office, even a powder room if there's enough stand-up space. Build custom-designed drawers that pull out through the wall. If you have stairs in or near your kitchen, use the space for extra kitchen storage—a pantry maybe?

Many people adorn stair walls with family photos or prized artwork because these expansive walls can be seen easily from throughout the room. For the same reason, these walls are a terrific spot to house a book collection.

CHAPTER FOUR

TRICKS OF THE TRADE

© Michael Garland/D & J Woodcraft, Inc. (both photos)

Left and above: One unexpected twist and an old organizing idea is new again. You'd probably never guess that this exquisite cabinet conceals an old-fashioned Murphy bed.

The road to do-it-yourself organization invariably passes through specialty stores, home-improvement centers, mail-order catalogs, and how-to books of all kinds (see the sources section at the back of the book). Traveling this road is essentially a commitment to retrofitting, or refitting, your existing spaces. I wish I could offer you an exhaustive list of the latest and greatest retrofitting products or tell you exactly where to shop. I can't. New products enter the race all the time and warehouse-style home-improvement chains seem to pop up overnight. Nonetheless, I present the following as inspiration for getting and staying organized. But first, a warning: Don't saw off more than you can rebuild.

DO-IT-YOURSELF PERSONALITY TYPES

Some handymen and -women fancy themselves more handy than their handiness would indicate. My clients often want to participate in organizing their homes, and many also ask me what work they can do themselves to save on construction costs. I answer with a straightforward question: What's your do-it-yourself personality?

TYPE A. Capable of small amounts of construction; familiar with basic tools and building terminology; can translate two-dimensional plans into three-dimensional construction. Example: If a kitchen cabinet has fixed shelves, type A successfully builds and installs slide-out trays.

TYPE B. Construction competent but not confident; prefers to buy exact product rather than build it; can install most elementary hardware. Example: Type B purchases a retail pull-out tray with glides and easily installs it under the shelf.

TYPE C. Zero construction literacy; prefers to contract out all home-improvement and repair work; will use a retail product to avoid construction. Example: Type C purchases turntable bins that will rest on shelf or hires carpenter to retrofit shelf with pull-out trays.

1 If commissioning custom-made furniture or storage pieces, have them built in sections so they can be rearranged and adapted to new space if you move or decide to use them elsewhere several years later.

2 Build kitchen and bathroom countertops to accommodate your height, especially if you're tall. The higher the counter, the more storage space at your disposal below. Don't, however, raise the counter height to an uncomfortable level simply in the interest of gaining more undercounter storage. Compensate in other ways.

3 Use stairways, hallways, and landings as found space.

Courtesy AristoKraft

Above: Don't overlook the insides of cabinet doors when you're squeezing out more storage inches. Retrofitting interior spaces is always a good idea. Above right: Think of stairs as found space, especially when they're adjacent to a small kitchen where pantry storage could be built beneath.

© Michael Garland/design by Alice Fellows

WHERE TO RETROFIT

Theoretically, any space in your home can be refitted to function better. Based on experience, however, I'd have to say that drawers, closets, and cabinets are the best for retrofitting using minor construction or retail products. The most popular improvement to these spaces? Pull-outs, of course! The secret to good pull-outs is in the glides.

Always buy full-extension glides so that your tray will completely extend. Be sure the model you're considering is suitable for its intended use and anticipated weight load.

Check, too, for safety stops that keep trays from falling out. Test the glide. Some are noisier than others; some glide more smoothly. All in all, get the best quality you can for your particular need. If the conditions are right, investigate two-way drawer glides so that your tray will slide open from either direction. These are especially nice for use on trays or drawers in kitchen islands or peninsulas. You can also buy self-closing glides. True, you do have to start the closing process with these mechanisms, but they will close gently, automatically, and completely once released. This type of

© Balthazar Korab

DOORWAY DILEMMAS

Standard doors can be space-planning terrors. Doors that are generally left open often obscure perfectly good wall space. The direction of their swing also affects space planning. Try to limit the intrusion of a door into a room, closet, or pantry if for no other reason than to get more floor space. Instead of a standard door, use two center-opening doors to close off the opening without covering up so much wall space behind the door. At the very least, change the door's swing to complement your space-planning needs.

Pocket doors that slide away into the wall have space-planning virtues, particularly in passages where you would normally keep the door open but want to use the wall space. I don't advise them for use in humid places, however, or wherever you open and close the door often.

Above left: A cornucopia of ideas for using modular storage systems to organize an existing or new closet. Left and far left (two views): What you don't use regularly, store out of the way but within reach. Lift-ups are perfect for specialty cooking gear.

Above: Cabinets with fixed shelves are prime candidates for retrofitting. With minimal installation, this unit creates a drawer in otherwise wasted height between shelves. Above right: Space planning happens on a small scale, too. A compact cutting center with a flip-down front poses as a drawer when closed and stores knives safely and within reach when open. Right: This kitchen corner is a perfect example of utilizing wall returns. A shallow cabinet and wine rack sandwiched between two doorways optimizes unused wall storage. The desk should be noted for the clever use of cubbies for holding frequently used papers.

glide is especially good for families with absentminded members who never manage to fully close anything!

You can also use drawer glides for more than just drawers. A pull-out tie rack or hanging pole are two additional options. The trick is to think about what you need and then find the hardware that will meet that need.

Yes, Virginia, there's more to retrofitting than pull-out trays. The preceding photographs illustrate only a few of the specialty items I often specify for clients who want to avoid major construction. Available at builders' or cabinetmakers' supply houses, these items are gems for increasing usable space and organizing your possessions.

AND NOW, A WORD ABOUT MATERIALS

The old adage says it best: You get what you pay for. Shelving constructed from less sturdy material may cost less, but over time, the shelves may sag. The better quality building material you use, the nicer and more durable the finished product will be. Bear in mind, quality doesn't always equal price. Whether you hire a professional space planner or shop for your retrofitting items yourself, evaluate all materials in light of your budget, your needs, and anticipated wear and tear.

For the most part, I recommend using prefinished materials (technically called high-pressure and low-pressure laminates) in closets as well as in the interiors of bathroom and kitchen drawers and cabinets. Not only does this save time—the material does not need painting or finishing—it generally looks nicer, too. Painting custom closets can be time-consuming with less-than-perfect results. There are so many shelves, nooks, and crannies. If you're investing in organized space, do it completely. Don't scrimp at the last minute.

MORE ON WOOD

Wood is beautiful building material. It adds a real sense of luxury to furniture, cabinets, and rooms. Because wood can be expensive, especially for custom fabrications, I suggest asking plenty of questions about what wood is right for your installation and budget. Keep in mind that most storage construction would call for plywood rather than solid wood. Here are a few starters.

The price of wood depends upon the type and the cut. In general, a rotary cut is less expensive than a plain slice. However, a plain slice cut is usually much more attractive than a rotary cut. The cut looks more uniform and compliments the wood's natural grain.

Moderately priced woods include oak, birch, some cherries, and rotary-cut mahogany. Walnut, maple, bird's-eye maple, and teak are considerably more costly, as they're more exotic woods. I find that a paint-grade birch, oak, or walnut is a good way to get the look and luxury of wood on a budget. It's my contention that more expensive woods should be reserved for the living room or other public room use. Why hide all that beauty behind closet doors?

I don't recommend soft pine; it's too easily dented and the knot holes tend to leach paint. On the topic of painting, fiberboard is suitable for painting, particleboard is not. Also, cedar is a rough wood. But if your heart's set on a cedar closet, ask for tongue-and-groove rather than panels.

© Michael Garland/D & J Woodcraft, Inc.

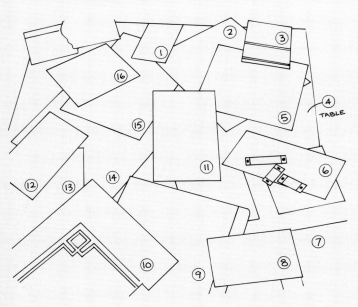

1 Plain slice maple is an inexpensive wood with consistent coloration and is similar to birch.

2 Plain slice cherry has a warm natural tone that looks elegant with clear finishes or deep stains.

3 Crotch mahogany with a satin wood border and ebony inlay presents a rich, traditional look.

4 Bird's-eye maple takes its name from the representative, natural swirl of the grain.

5 Figured African mahogany has a natural wave that reflects light beautifully.

6 Pre-dyed woods such as white-dyed anagre come in a range of luxurious, saturated colors.

7 Anagre finished with a medium stain creates an exotic look.

8 Zebra wood has a unique heavy gold-and-black-striped appearance.

9 Mappa French maple burl reveals distinctive characteristics of the tree. This piece is accented with curly maple.

10 Black American walnut, the all-around "nice guy" of woods, shown with oriental front work.

11 This wood was antiqued and distressed to purposely create a well-aged feel.

12 Another paint finish from the family of "antique makers" is the crackle finish shown here.

13 A stained finish on this sample of ebonized quartered ash emphasizes the wood's natural color.

14 Historically, bird's-eye maple was used during the 1950s and the art deco period of home furnishings.

15 Quartered sapele mahogany has a narrow straight grain, which is nice for traditional-style woodwork, vertical applications, or accents.

16 Pre-dyed lacewood veneers are available in blues, pinks, greens, ivories, and other hues for unusual wood pieces.

ORGANIZING
ROOM BY ROOM

KITCHENS, PANTRIES, AND DINING ROOMS

Left: Dual islands organize this kitchen into activity centers. An overhead pot rack, glass-front cabinets, and a mirrored backsplash create a feeling of openness. Above: Maximize dining room storage by mixing built-ins with space-intensive cabinets.

Mmm. The pleasure of working in an attractive space-efficient kitchen. Oh, the delight of opening a well-designed double-height cabinet or walk-in pantry that almost wantonly displays its contents to you. Ah, the wonderful anticipation that comes with gathering around the dining room table while tempting dish after tempting dish is carried in from the kitchen. It's enough to make Norman Rockwell blush.

But beware. Behind this dream kitchen, this bountiful pantry, this Americana dining room could lurk...clutter. And, dare I say it... wasted space!

There's only one surefire way to protect yourself from these culinary demons: Organize! Your kitchen, pantry (or whatever functions as one in your house), and dining room form links in the same chain. They'll function only as well as the weakest link. If your pantry is inefficient and poorly planned, chances are your kitchen suffers a similar fate. A disorganized kitchen hampers meal preparation and entertaining, which could make the dining experience less enjoyable. The following pages feature many fresh ideas for tackling kitchen-related clutter.

KITCHENS

Every member of the family—Spot and Snowball included—uses the kitchen at least once during the course of an average day. How many other rooms in your house see this much activity on a daily basis? At various times during the day, your kitchen may be a classroom, practice hall, indoor soccer arena, office, makeshift doctor's office, or traffic-control tower. Your kitchen is your home's laboratory, its heart and soul, and potentially, its strongest selling point. For all these reasons and more, your kitchen should be the most carefully thought-out, planned, and organized room in your house.

Architect: Marvin Ullman & Associates, Chicago, IL/Interior Design: Christine Garrett, Evanston, IL/Photo: Ellis of Jessie Walker Associates

Kitchen pass-throughs are underrated. This design visually separates the kitchen from other rooms, creates a fifth wall for attractive storage, and provides a small counter for after-school snacks, buffet-style serving, or socializing during dinner parties.

FORM AND FUNCTION

This is why in the kitchen, more than anywhere else, form should follow function. Most kitchens, even the tiniest of rooms, are quite complex, owing to the variety of tasks performed there. Kitchens are also highly personal rooms. Every cook honors his or her own techniques, types of equipment, lighting, decor, surfacing materials, even window treatments. In addition, both gourmet cooks and experts in the art of microwaving come in all heights, shapes, and sizes. Some are right-handed, others left. All of these differences should be accounted for in the kitchen in order to make the cooking, serving, and dining experience as pleasurable and safe as possible.

Start planning your kitchen by first evaluating your needs, just as you would when planning any other room of the house. The list on page 50 contains several "kitchen questions" you should ask yourself. With each kitchen I work on, both new construction and remodels, I begin by asking the client to consider these issues. We also discuss aesthetics and style preferences, although the project architect or interior designer typically addresses these concerns. The space planner concentrates on the

details, such as how many pots, pans, and appliances versus silver trays and serving pieces need to be stored and how activities and traffic patterns will impact storage needs.

When you consider all the factors involved in space planning and organizing a kitchen, there's so much valuable information that it's hard to decide where to begin. Perhaps it's best to start with a caveat. As you peruse my suggestions, please keep in mind that ideas for kitchen planning and organization may be gleaned from anywhere—especially if you allow yourself to be flexible and to think unconventionally. A pen-and-pencil carousel designed for office use, for example, might make a perfect place to store and organize small kitchen gadgets.

Although entire books have been devoted to the topic, the ideas that follow are from my own years of hands-on organizing and space planning for clients with all types of unique needs. Consider these suggestions a combination of common sense and experience. Start with the basic ingredients—configuration and layout—then season to taste with decor, materials, and lighting preferences. Bake according to your budget, and presto, an organized kitchen.

Accomplished "chefs" may wish to add an island or peninsula for texture. Yes, I can almost smell that satisfying feeling of having the ideal kitchen. Ready to sample? Let's get cookin'!

LAYOUTS AND CONFIGURATIONS

The hallmark of today's kitchens is individuality, usually that of the principal user with a hint of the architect's or certified kitchen designer's (CKD) thrown in. But what truly sets a kitchen apart, what distinguishes one from another, is functionality. Some kitchens, just like people, function better than others.

While much has been said about a kitchen "work triangle," or the positioning of the sink, the stove or range, and the refrigerator at the points of a triangle with counters and work surfaces completing the geometry, other options exist. Incorporating activity-specific "work centers" into kitchen designs has proven quite successful, especially with the proliferation of two-cook households. The fundamental principle behind both layouts is traffic flow.

A well-configured kitchen should facilitate movement and activity. Think about where you enter with groceries, where groceries are unloaded, where food is stored, where meals are cooked and eaten, and where dishes are done. How you interact with the machines or elements in your kitchen determines the room's overall efficiency. The design community refers to this interaction as "ergonomics."

Besides being an oft-quoted buzz word, ergonomics is the relationship of people to machines in order to maximize work efficiency. An ergonomic chair is, theoretically, so comfortable that it actually enhances your ability to type, write, draft, or even think. Following the analogy, an ergonomic kitchen is one that enhances your ability to function efficiently in that space as you interact with its contents. Once you understand how you and your family move about your kitchen, the most ergonomic (and safest) configurations should suggest themselves to you. At the very least, you ought to realize what patterns to avoid. While you're visualizing, allow me to draw yet another picture.

ISLANDS AND PENINSULAS

Does your kitchen have a mind of its own? Do gadgets, utensils, and thingamajigs spontaneously explode from your cabinets and

Environmental responsibility places an additional burden on household storage space. What used to be discarded is now accumulated—in our kitchens, pantries, utility rooms, garages, and porches—and then recycled. Fortunately, there are currently several options for custom, built-in receptacles as well as many attractive and efficient retail products. But just because product manufacturers are making recycling more convenient, don't forget the goal. Remember to take recyclables to the appropriate places on a regular basis; transporting them from your kitchen recycling bin to your garage to your trunk doesn't accomplish much.

Above left: Kitchen geography—islands and peninsulas—gave this client more work space and activity-specific storage areas. Above: Pull-out recycling bins conceal good ecological habits.

Top right: Space planning goes diagonal. A slanted island facilitates traffic flow in this client's kitchen. Bottom right: This tip-out holds sponges and the adjustable shelves are positioned precisely to fit contents. Opposite (two views): These same clients did not require a kitchen table. Reclaiming that area generated room for this custom nook, which I carefully space planned to tuck into a shallow, sun-filled alcove. The art-adorned sitting area features pull-out storage, a mini-desk, bookshelves, and a wall-mounted TV.

drawers every time you turn your back? Fret no more. I have just the cure. Take five walls and call me in the morning!

Fortunately, this prescription is not as ludicrous as it sounds. Essentially, I'm suggesting that you add an island or peninsula to your kitchen. For anyone who's ever wished they had one more wall, a configuration that includes either of these structures is ideal. When wall space runs out, an island or peninsula solves several problems. They separate kitchen activities and provide additional work surfaces. They present an area for informal dining or children's arts-and-crafts projects, not to mention extra storage!

The pictures on these pages are only a few ways islands and peninsulas can spice up your recipe for an organized dream kitchen. Remember, think unconventionally. Islands don't have to be square or rectangular; peninsulas don't have to be at ninety degrees to their anchor counter or wall. Both could curve or angle in whatever direction best suits your kitchen and space-planning needs.

KITCHEN DECOR: PERSONALITY, PANACHE, AND PERFORMANCE

Kitchen decor, whether country fresh or city-slick futuristic, should please you without interfering with the room's main function: food storage and meal preparation. As we discussed earlier, some decorative styles can limit practicality by usurping usable inches or consuming too much floor space. While your personal tastes will (and should!) influence

the style of your kitchen, keep a watchful eye out for appliances, furniture, or styling that dictate storage space. You, not your belongings or your decor, make the decision as to what goes where.

No one kitchen style or decor outshines another. But there are a few points worth mentioning. One design technique I do recommend is an architectural decision I once saw described as "skyscraping," which takes full advantage of the room's height by building cabinets or shelves right up to the ceiling. High shelves are good places to store occasionally used utensils or dishes. If you decide that skyscraping is not for you, then remember that cabinet tops can double as ideal display cases.

Granted, not every aspect of kitchen decor directly impacts space planning and organization. Lighting and surfacing materials, for example, don't in and of themselves yield more storage space, but they do enhance your kitchen's efficiency. Thus, you can stay better organized. The sidebar on this page lists other decor checkpoints to consider when planning an organized kitchen.

DECOR DOS AND DON'TS

■ Do make yourself top priority. Choose a decor that compliments your taste and cooking style. Build countertops below your bent elbow height for maximum comfort. Your physical well-being is important when working in the kitchen.

■ Do install windows that open either up or out. Don't cut into your work or storage space with windows that tilt in toward you.

■ Do select single drawer pulls designed for the center of the drawer so you can easily access the contents with a gentle pull from one hand.

■ Don't overlook heating, ventilation, air-conditioning (HVAC), and mechanical needs. Where electrical, gas, and plumbing supply lines lie within your kitchen will affect storage capacity.

■ Don't forget banquettes. Window seats and boothlike dining tables are at home in any decor and provide additional storage space when drawers are built in beneath the seat.

■ Do match materials to function. If a less appealing surfacing material is the best choice for a chopping area, dress up the look with a decorative backsplash. Conversely, limit marble, an expensive and extremely porous material, to the baking center, where it's most functional.

■ Do prioritize lighting. Lighting designers and manufacturers have masterfully responded to the call for decorative but functional task lighting. Don't install lighting that casts shadows over your work surface.

CHILD SAFETY

Curious children of all ages like to experiment with gadgets and gizmos, especially if they see Mom or Dad using them, but putting things out of Junior's reach can sabotage kitchen organization unless safety concerns are accounted for in the initial space planning. There are several precautions you can take to make your kitchen child-friendly and organized. Here are a few ideas.

■ Centrally store knives and sharp objects in drawers with childproof latches, which are sold in most hardware stores.

■ Knives can also be stored in custom-made slots at the back of the counter or in the top of the backsplash where blades can be tucked away safely.

■ Use cabinet doors with self-closing glides so kids won't bump into doors accidentally left open.

■ Add safety catches to keep drawers from spilling if opened too far.

■ Designate a drawer, shelf, or entire area in your kitchen to store children's snacks, plates, utensils, and so on. Be sure to include appropriate seating.

Courtesy Crystal Cabinet Works, Inc.

Above: A child-safe knife organizer. Right: Thoughtful space planning maximized storage at every level of this kitchen without crowding the room's decor. Notice how a peninsula balances the "fifth-wall" cabinets.

KITCHEN QUESTIONS

Space planners make it their business to zero in on the details that are so critical to obtaining and maintaining an organized kitchen. As you answer the following questions—and these are only a few!—you'll realize that no detail is superfluous.

PHYSICAL ATTRIBUTES

■ Are you right- or left-handed?

■ How tall are you?

■ Do you prefer to sit or stand when working in the kitchen?

■ How high can you comfortably reach?

FOOD PREPARATION

■ How many cooks use the kitchen and how often?

■ Do your children prepare their own snacks?

■ What type of cooking do you generally do?

■ Do you squeeze fresh orange juice every morning or grab a glass on the way out?

■ Which appliances do you use all the time?

■ Do you plan on acquiring any specialized equipment?

■ What types of appliances do you own: gas, electric, commercial?

■ Do caterers often come into your kitchen?

Courtesy Rutt Custom Cabinetry

Courtesy Crystal Cabinet Works, Inc.

Courtesy Lillian Vernon

© Michael Garland

Courtesy NuTone

Courtesy Lillian Vernon

© Appleton, Mechur & Associates, architects, photo by Michael Garland/Maxine Ordesky, space design

WAYS TO REORGANIZE WITHOUT RESTRUCTURING

Even without the resources or inclination to remodel your kitchen, you can "respace-plan" by either purchasing storage helpers or simply rethinking how you use your kitchen. Here are some ideas.

RETHINK:

1. Place table accessories—napkins, dinnerware, place mats—in one place near the dinner table.
2. Establish a staging area with paper, pencil, phone, phone numbers, calendar, grocery list, and so on.
3. Notice and eliminate extra steps. Place everything you need for a specific activity near the area where you do that task.
4. Put large or less-used cookware on higher shelves.
5. Use a rolling step stool for access.
6. Clear the counters of appliances (or stuff) you don't use every day.

PURCHASE:

1. In-drawer or on-shelf organizers.
2. Under-shelf and under-cabinet organizers.
3. Bins designed to hang on the inside of cabinet doors.
4. Ready-made pull-outs for use under the sink and in other cabinets.
5. Turntables for cabinets, pantries, and even your fridge.
6. Hooks to hang baskets or shelves from the ceiling.
7. A rolling butcher-block or microwave cart with storage space.
8. Track-mounted shelves to hang on unused wall space.
9. Freestanding storage units to fill wasted space in corners or under windows.

Top: Custom storage flanks the breakfast area in this client's kitchen; a step-down island holds books while a built-in wall unit behind the table features concealed and glass-front closed storage. The basket collection is displayed nicely atop cabinets. Bottom: A sampling of items for retrofitting kitchen storage.

■ Do you stock up on groceries on a monthly basis and fill in weekly with fresh meats and produce or do you shop "European style" on an as-needed basis?

■ Do you require any special equipment, such as a hearth oven?

■ Do you need specific counter surfaces for making candy, breads, or pastry?

■ What items need to be stored safely out of children's reach?

EATING AND ENTERTAINING

■ Do you eat in the kitchen? At a table or counter?

■ How often do you eat in your kitchen?

■ Does everyone in your family eat at the same time?

■ Do you entertain frequently?

■ How many people do you usually host?

■ Is your wet bar in your kitchen?

■ Do young children require any special accommodations?

CLEANUP AND STORAGE

■ Who generally does the dishes?

■ Do you keep your food in the kitchen or store things in an auxiliary room?

■ Do you have more than one refrigerator and freezer?

OTHER ACTIVITIES

■ Do children do homework in the kitchen?

■ Do you pay your bills at a kitchen desk?

■ Is the family TV in the kitchen?

■ Do you wrap gifts on the kitchen table?

■ Is your kitchen the starting point for your children's arts-and-crafts projects?

■ Is your fridge your home's art gallery?

■ Do you give cooking classes or demonstrations?

COOKING WITHOUT
CHAOS

Here's a quick hit list of organizing techniques for keeping chaos out of the kitchen.

■ Use drawer dividers or stacking silverware trays for large or deep drawers.

■ Maximize counter top space by using caddies, decorative but practical jars, and knife holders.

■ Take advantage of wall space with shelves, pegboard, and hanging organizers.

■ Retrofit deep cabinets with pull-out trays and corner cabinets with turntables.

■ Store things nearest to where you use them.

■ Keep spices by category or alphabetically.

■ Store infrequently used items in upper cabinets or out of the kitchen.

■ Buy and use a rolling step stool.

■ Double shelf space by attaching under-shelf, plastic-covered wire baskets and shelves or by using ready-made products that hold and display small items at different heights.

Courtesy Crystal Cabinet Works, Inc (top three photos)

POTS AND PANS

The only thing more annoying than listening to someone bang pots and pans looking for what they need is doing it yourself! Keep pots and pans near the cooking center; since lids aren't always used, they can be separately stored in upright positions and grouped by size or cookware. While I'm on the subject of things used in or on the stove and oven, what about going for the full-restaurant look if you already have a commercial cook top or range? Customize your counter near the stove to hold a spring-loaded plate dispenser. You gotta admit it's a conversation piece and you could reclaim the cabinet shelf for something else. Custom-designed or custom-tailored drawers under cook tops are the ideal place.

COOKBOOKS

If you're lucky enough to have your favorite recipes memorized or preserved on your computer, you won't have to worry about storing cookbooks. Most of us, however, are always looking for somewhere handy to keep them. Ideally your cookbooks should all be together and near where you use them. I have found that one of the most convenient places is on adjustable bookshelves built into a kitchen island or a wall near or beside the door. Don't overlook the space between your cabinet tops and the ceiling, especially if you're not skyscraping your kitchen.

The next trick is working with them. One particularly clever way to make room for an

Above right (from left): Wood inserts for beverage drawers; a custom-built, on-door spice rack; pull-out plastic bins attached under shelf. Right: This basic organizer for pots and pans has movable hooks and room for matching lids. The plate rail above completes the look and utilizes valuable wall space.

RETROFITTED REFRIGERATOR

© Maxine Ordesky

VINYL-COATED 3-TIER STEP-UP SHELVES FOR SMALL ITEMS

VINYL-COATED "RISER" RACKS TO PROVIDE SHELF FOR ICE CUBE TRAYS AND SMALL THINGS

SMALL TURNTABLE FOR JAMS, MUSTARD, RELISH, ETC.

PLASTIC BIN TO HOLD MILK (IN CASE OF LEAKAGE)

LARGE TURNTABLE FOR MELONS, ORANGES, GRAPEFRUITS, ETC.

VINYL-COATED SOFT DRINK DISPENSER

STORE-BOUGHT PLASTIC TUBS FOR ADDITIONAL VEGETABLES

BUILT-IN CRISPER DRAWER

Courtesy Crystal Cabinet Works, Inc.

open cookbook near your work surface is to build a pull-out (or pull-down) tray to hold it. You might also consider buying one of several specially designed cookbook holders. You could also design your backsplash to accommodate open cookbooks.

CONFIGURATIONS

Think of your kitchen as a new suit or dress, and your space planner as your tailor. Although conventional kitchen wisdom holds sway over most kitchens—appliances are

where you expect them to be and counters, islands, or peninsulas are boring old box shapes—you can still make sure the final product is custom made to fit you. Space planning means planning the space—exactly and innovatively.

ISLANDS AND PENINSULAS

My kingdom for an island! There are so many wonderful ways to utilize islands—and peninsulas—in kitchens. Again, think unconventionally. Even a small island or peninsula may be worth building if you gain extra storage and a secondary work surface.

FOUND SPACE

A lack of organization is often due to a lack of space. After all, you can't truly organize your kitchen without enough space. But what do you do if you can't remodel, can't change a structural thing about your kitchen? You go on a space hunt. Let me show you the way.

Top left: These days, space planning can be refrigerated. Fortunately, appliance manufacturers are designing smarter and more organized refrigerators with tip-out bins, adjustable shelves, and compartmentalized storage. However, you can also organize an existing fridge by retrofitting it with inexpensive, readily available items. The nice thing about this space-planning technique is that you can customize your cold storage to suit your needs and life-style. This drawing illustrates several useful ideas. I particularly like turntables. Bottom left: This under-counter pull-down cookbook holder is easily installed and saves lots of space.

LOST SPACE

Most kitchens suffer from "gaposis," the ailment of lost space between large appliances and between appliances and cabinetry. Curing gaposis is as simple as converting or reclaiming the in-between space to hold tall, narrow items that can be stored vertically. Although these plans are not complete building instructions, they do illustrate this solution. If possible, use rolling storage rather than built-in so you can remove the unit if you buy an even larger appliance. Filling in these gaps also adds bonus counter space, but remember to match or line up your new cabinets with those already in the room.

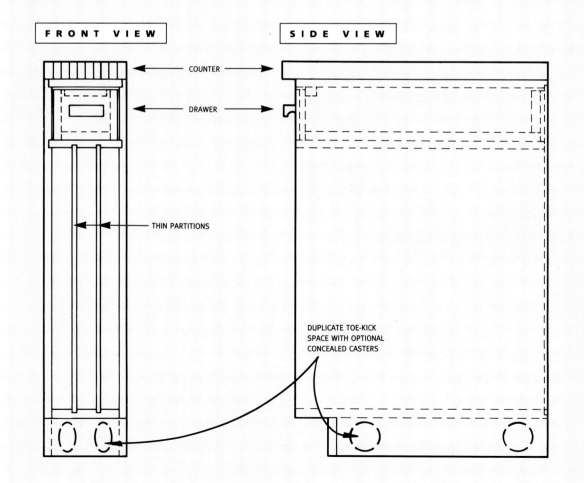

FRONT VIEW **SIDE VIEW**

From 50 Storage Ideas For the Home by Kate Armpriester and Mary Jane Favorite

PANTRIES

Whenever I wax poetic about space planning, I can't help but wonder why the butler's pantry is a thing of the past. It seems to have vanished right along with the butler. Like so many things from the good ol' days, the concept of a butler's pantry was a space planner's delight.

Traditionally, it was a small room strategically situated in the passageway that connected the kitchen to the dining room. In it, dishes, flatware, linens, silver serving pieces, food, beverages, and only the butler knew what else were easily stored in an organized manner. Some even had sinks and functioned as mini-kitchens. Without that room, however, today's homes typically squeeze all of those items into smaller kitchens and smaller dining rooms.

A client who entertains often needed two pantries: an updated butler's pantry (above) with storage, sink, dishwasher, desk, and file drawers; and a food pantry (left), which I fitted with shelves, pull-outs, a work surface, and door-activated lighting.

© Michael Garland/Maxine Ordesky, space design

Well, I'm here to sing the virtues of pantries, pantries of all sizes and all shapes. I always tell my clients that the secret to being organized, especially in the kitchen, is planning a space that enables them to function in a more efficient manner. A pantry—whether it's a separate room, a freestanding cabinet, or shallow shelves built into the wall—allows the whole kitchen to be more functional. A well-designed and well-utilized pantry should hold everything while still displaying its contents to you at a glance, making it easier for you to find and reach what you want without a lot of needless hunting, bending, or juggling.

As I said, a pantry can be almost anywhere: in an adjacent garage, beneath stairs, even on the walls leading down to the basement. What about the kitchen window or eating alcove that, thanks to urban sprawl, no longer has a pleasant view? You could turn it into your butler's pantry complete with natural lighting.

The photographs shown here are only a sampling of how you can create a pantry in your kitchen. Remember, your goals are visibility and accessibility. To that end, use pull-out or rotating shelves whenever possible. Be flexible, too. Adjustable shelves allow you to reorganize your pantry as your needs change, say during holiday seasons, when cooking and baking may triple.

Nowadays, retail and custom-manufactured cabinet companies are giving the pantry its due. In addition to many retail products available for retrofitting existing shelves or outgrown pantry space, you can also buy entire cabinets to install as new pantries.

DINING ROOMS

The great American dining room has always been more than that. My father-in-law, an accountant, ran his business from his dining room table. And when my own home-based enterprise occasionally demanded a larger work force, we, too, spread out on the dining room table. The smooth expanse of a large dining room table invites so many activities

Above: I stocked this small, step-in wall pantry with space planning, including wraparound adjustable shelves, a deep pull-out container, on-door bins, and organized floor storage. Right: A stepped organizer elevates small jars.

Courtesy Lilian Vernon

other than dining: sewing, homework, office- or home-related paperwork, arts and crafts, card or game playing.

Traditionally, dining rooms were separate rooms in the home, reserved for formal meals and special family occasions. Much to my disappointment, we're in danger of losing our dining rooms. In today's space-conscious homes, separate formal dining rooms are often sacrificed for family rooms, big eat-in kitchens, or larger living rooms. It's too bad,

because dining rooms are full of storage potential.

More often than not, dining rooms are underutilized with respect to storage and organization, partially because of the nature of the room and the lack of functional space planning. People seem to prefer their dining rooms to be open and to feel uncluttered; it does make entertaining nicer. But remember, separate dining rooms do not have continuous traffic flow. So, with the right furniture

The book shelves flanking this formal dining area make excellent use of existing architecture and create a pleasant ambiance. Soffit lighting delicately illuminates the collection of books and china.

In homes where the dining room occasionally or routinely doubles as office space, here's a theoretical representation of how you can modify or customize a buffet to accommodate both work and home storage needs. The idea, of course, is to hide the cabinet's dual personality behind the exterior. Simply looking at the closed view (top) you'd never imagine what the cabinet concealed (bottom). I've space planned this buffet to hold a fax machine, filing drawers, pull-out trays, and palettes for stationery and envelopes. Crystal and china are displayed conventionally.

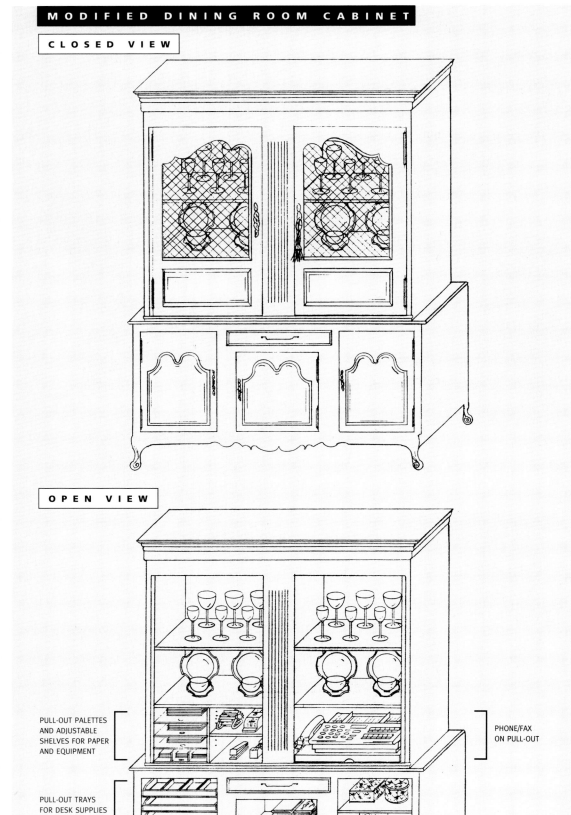

MODIFIED DINING ROOM CABINET

CLOSED VIEW

OPEN VIEW

PULL-OUT PALETTES AND ADJUSTABLE SHELVES FOR PAPER AND EQUIPMENT

PHONE/FAX ON PULL-OUT

PULL-OUT TRAYS FOR DESK SUPPLIES

LATERAL FILE DRAWER

© Maxine Ordesky

and good space planning, a dining room can be all things to all people.

SERVING UP MORE SPACE IN THE DINING ROOM

If your dining room hasn't yet gone the way of the disappearing butler and his pantry, there are certain things you should have in there to make it more efficient. For instance, a cabinet or piece of furniture traditionally known as a buffet or sideboard is not only ideal for serving food and beverages during mealtime, but it also gives you plenty of space to store silver, linens, serving pieces, wine, and so on. If your dining room is also your office, buffets and sideboards can be modified to hold filing drawers or shelves.

You can purchase many well-made retail or custom-manufactured dining room buffets or sideboards. But in order to truly organize your dining room without encroaching on its ambiance, work with a space planner to custom-design innovative space and storage solutions.

A pass-through from the kitchen is also a good feature in a dining room. It can help you stay organized when serving meals and, as a bonus, often brings in more light to both rooms. If the area is large enough, you may even want to build a ledge, with or without closed shelving, beneath the pass-through or along a wall for extra work, display, and storage space.

Another way to better utilize dining room space is to build bookshelves or custom storage units into side wall returns. Under some conditions, you may even be able to incorporate the door from the dining room to the kitchen into this unit for a truly custom look. Don't overlook the space beneath dining room windows, either. This is a good place to build custom benches or cabinets that offer extra storage room, display space for decorative items, or informal seating.

Building open shelves behind doors also capitalizes on underused space without encroaching on the room's feeling of openness. And of course, we can't neglect the ubiquitous plate rail. Dining rooms are ideal places for these storage gold mines.

Overall, I'd have to say the number one secret to organizing dining rooms is to think how you can customize your room's quirks—and your own—to turn open space into item- or need-specific storage space.

Left and above: Trompe l'oeil chair backs and legs complete the picture-perfect decor of this elegant dining room, drawing the eye away from the upholstered bench. This artistic approach is a terrific solution for concealing or integrating storage into any room.

Design: Ruschman Elliot Interior Design, Winnetka Ill/Photo: Mikos of Jessie Walker & Associates (both photos)

CHAPTER TWO

LIVING AND FAMILY ROOMS

© Bill Rothschild/Michael Orsini & Judith Leventhon, interior design

© Michael Garland/design by Allie Chang Paul (both photos)

Left: Shelving above the couch introduces considerable book storage to a family room that previously had none. Above: Two views of a custom media cabinet designed for optimum accessibility. Drawer inserts organize CDs and cassettes.

Although much has been written about the Victorian era, one of the Victorians' more creative and valuable contributions to modern-day society has been overlooked: the parlor, the precursor to our own living rooms. The parlor was the one room in the Victorian home that was reserved exclusively for receiving guests. Day-to-day living took place elsewhere throughout the house. Although the traditional parlor had survived for many centuries, it too suffered under the weight of the Great Depression.

In some communities, families retreated to running businesses from their homes in search of work and income, and the parlor became their storefront, shop, and office. Formal entertaining took a backseat—and a back room. The kitchen and other rooms absorbed the added pressure of receiving guests and fulfilling intended roles. Perhaps domestic Darwinism took hold and somewhere along the line the family room evolved as the stronger offspring of the living room and kitchen.

The family room became just that—a room for the family to gather in—and remains true to its origins. So true, in fact, that families with both rooms congregate in the family room almost to the exclusion of the living room, except of course when "real" company comes. In these homes, the living room generally doesn't require much planning with respect to storage and organizing. In this case, the desire for an organized living room is more display driven than storage driven.

In homes without family rooms, the living room does double duty; electronics meet antiques, children's games meet parents' art collections. A great deal of space-planning attention must be paid to this all-purpose room to make it functional for users of all ages.

Families keep a variety of things in family rooms and therefore need to employ a variety of space-planning techniques. A good method is to utilize the wall space between and below windows. Even the corner of this room is maximized for storage.

THE TRUTH ABOUT LIVING ROOMS

I'll start with the easier task, space-planning what I'll term a *true* living room. As I suggested, most people don't store things in their living rooms as much as they display them. I've often wondered whether or not people judge one another on the basis of their living rooms. The Victorians certainly did. Maybe that's why true living rooms are much like dining rooms: elegant but terrifically underutilized with respect to their storage potential.

Before I go any further, let me say that I have no quarrel with anyone who prefers their dining or living room to feel open or be unencumbered by storage pieces. That's great if it works for you. My goal is not to convert you into space-hunting junkies but to help you find more space if you want it. Now, back to the living room.

STORAGE OR STYLE— WHY NOT BOTH?

The easiest way to maximize living room storage space—and exercise personal taste—is with bookcases and furniture. Bookcases come in so many shapes, sizes, and styles that you can put them anywhere. The most underused spot in living rooms is between and/or beneath windows. Identical bookcases positioned between several windows will increase storage and display room without detracting from the room's ambiance. Similarly, built-in bookcases that surround the room also maximize living room storage. The advantage of custom bookcases or wall units that go all the way up to the ceiling is that they become part of the room's decor and can even be designed to look like walls. Others tuck neatly away in otherwise wasted space.

Trunks, chests, and similar pieces work very well as coffee table bases or end tables. If you're lucky enough to own an antique

In space planning a family room in a California Craftsman Bungalow-style home, I deferred to the architecture and used custom cabinets of figured cherry wood. An adjustable bookshelf (top left) has pull-outs for games and a copper-lined firewood bin. The media cabinet (two views above) was angled for TV viewing. An antique chest (left), a real catch by interior designer Carol Poet, hides sleeping bags.

biblioteque or armoire, it might be a good place to stow a television in your living room, in addition to books, games, photo albums, and so on. Of course, custom pieces are the best way to get the right combination of living room storage and display space, but it also helps to buy smart. Look for coffee tables, for example, that offer closed storage space in addition to a pleasing design.

Don't forget about piano benches and hassocks as possible living room storage. For that matter, any upholstered stool or bench could have concealed storage under its lift-up seat or top. This type of functional, decorative storage works exceptionally well in the living room. Finally, rearrange your furniture as a means of organizing your living room. Bookcases and other freestanding pieces can be positioned as dividers to separate sections of your living room and provide storage.

You could also keep your audio equipment, records, or CDs out of sight but within reach. Place these items in a low bookcase cabinet that is positioned behind a couch. The couch stylishly camouflages the equipment and serves as the focal point for your

living room's conversation area. Voilà! You've space planned your living room! By the way, low cabinets and tables placed behind couches are also great places to "hide" magazines, books, or games.

Most people who have a true living room don't really need or want to organize it in the same way they want to organize a more frequently used room, such as a kitchen or bathroom. But a living room that's also a family room demands organization or it won't work well as either.

Above: The back wall of the same family room has identical bookcases and drawers under the window to avoid blocking natural light. Right: Store audio and video cassettes in custom pull-out trays (pictured) or in partitioned inserts.

FAMILY ROOM STORAGE

Wouldn't it be swell if your living room/family room worked like the Bat Cave, and by simply pushing a button, you could rotate the scene like Batman did on TV? Nice idea, but I doubt Gotham City's crime-fighting duo ever battled villains such as TVs, board games, toys, magazines, books, wall art, stereos, photo albums, vacuum cleaners, sewing machines.... You get the picture. But with a little space planning, you can *BOP! ZIFF! KAZOW!* your family room into shape.

Earlier, I said part of good organization is retrievability. Of course, it's always nice when things are easy to reach, especially for children. But the trick to organizing a family room, or any room that's used by the whole family for different purposes, is making it easy to keep organized and presentable. Kids will always find a way to reach what they want but they seem to lose their ingenuity when it comes to putting away those same items. Family room storage should be uncomplicated, almost automatic, so kids don't have to work at keeping it organized. In other words, make family room storage a simple one-step process.

One simple example of this principle is to avoid stacking board games too high. If kids have to reposition the entire stack every time they want to play a game, they'll never put the boxes away properly. The same phenomenon occurs, hard as it may be to believe, with adults. Games can be stored on pull-out or fixed shelves, in wall cabinets, or even taken out of their boxes and put into clear, stackable plastic containers to be stored on shelves. If all else fails—or is full—games

When one space plays dual roles, as this room does, organization takes center-stage. Conscientious space planning mixed with creativity yielded colorful cubbies for open storage and drawers below. The mantel shelf displays artwork.

WHICH CAME FIRST?
THE TV OR THE
FAMILY ROOM?

We may never know the answer to that question, but what is evident is that the family room revolves around the television (and Nintendo in many homes). Major storage and organizing decisions depend especially upon the sizes and shapes of your audio/visual equipment. For example, oversize rear-projection TVs must be on or near the floor for the best picture. But they also require ventilation, as does all electronic equipment. Electronic video games come with lots of cables and pieces. If you can arrange for storage of everything on one pull-out tray for example, you can keep the game hooked up and ready to go and make it easy to put away.

Because technology becomes obsolete so quickly these days, even the best-designed family room could be antiquated with the next generation of TVs. Consequently, you should know the specifications and exact dimensions of your TV, stereo, and electronic games before space planning your family room. Whether you plan to purchase or commission a wall unit, it should have some flexibility so that you and your wallet can keep pace with home-entertainment technology!

Design: Betty Jo Purvis/Photo: Mikos of Jessie Walker & Associates

Above right: Wall cabinets in family rooms hide games very well. The two-tier coffee table combines a playing surface with convenient storage. Right: Coffee tables with drawers are like oysters with pearls: hard to find but worth the hunt.

Photo: Ellis of Jessie Walker & Associates

could even be slipped under the sofa or, better yet, placed on the bookcases concealed by the sofa.

Ready-made products work well in family rooms, because you can buy exactly the right item for a specific purpose. Wall units are storage windfalls in the family room. In fact, one entire wall of any family room should be storage, in the form of purchased modular wall units or custom-built pieces. Of course a family room also needs seating and playing areas, but a full wall of storage allows ample room for electronics, books, music, artwork, and so on. Remember, too, the old living room trick of using trunks and chests as storage-rich coffee tables and end tables.

SOUND ADVICE

The same storage ideas suggested for dining rooms apply to living and family rooms. In the latter, however, you may also want to accommodate audio/visual equipment and computer games. True electronic aficionados, who have the space, store their high-tech equipment in special media rooms. But those of us who want to play the occasional CD or videotape a favorite movie have less complex storage needs.

In this case, custom-built media cabinets or even what's known as custom-manufactured storage systems work remarkably well. Modular wall units designed to hold audio/visual equipment, tapes, records, and CDs are available from a variety of retail and mail-order sources. There are also such items as metal-strip dividers and plastic trays designed to hold CDs, tapes, and videos upright within drawers. Other available items include cabinets with pop-up or pull-out platforms for concealing and revealing televisions and bookcase-style units sized to hold CDs or tapes.

I know what you're thinking. You're shaking your head and thinking, No way can I put electronics behind closed doors. The remote won't work. Not true. Now there are devices that will relay electronic signals from your remote right through such barriers as cabinet doors to your stereo (see sources at the back of the book). All you have to do is place these electronic genies on the storage unit or somewhere between you and your electronics.

Courtesy Häfele

© Gary Quesada/Balthazar Korab Ltd

Above: A sleek, custom-manufactured media cabinet with adjustable shelves holds home electronics and has top-shelf storage for videos and CDs. Left: These metal-strip dividers are an affordable, practical solution for organizing videos, cassettes, and CDs. Once in place, they're permanent and sturdy. They're also available in plastic.

CHAPTER THREE

BATHROOMS

Courtesy Robern

© Jessie Walker

Left: Small can be very organized. Equipping this bathroom with a multi-drawered pullman, mirrored cabinets, and a magazine niche yielded a myriad of storage areas. Above: Placement-and-use towel storage reclaims wasted space.

Bathrooms: the last frontier. Well, that may be a tad extreme, but they are possibly the sole remaining bastion of privacy in today's hustling, bustling households. It's almost ironic, too, because bathrooms, especially master baths, are so often a main attraction in many homes. Baths are arguably the most frequently remodeled room, perhaps second only to the kitchen. In fact, improving an existing bathroom or adding another is one of the few home-improvement projects that will pay for itself at resale time.

Good space planning will keep your small bathroom from being a washout, both from the standpoint of personal pleasure and fiscal foresight. It's worth showering your bath with a little attention. Remember the space-planning motto: the more efficient the space, the more enjoyable the experience.

A well-planned bathroom means never having to say excuse me. Two people should be able to occupy the space simultaneously without interfering with one another. That doesn't necessarily imply a sizable room. There are ways to space plan any bathroom so that it can comfortably accommodate more than one user. For instance, organize the space so that you can reach whatever you need at the sink from the sink. Stretching is a no-no. And leaving the room to get something that you regularly use in the bathroom breaks the space-planning golden rule of placement and use: Store things where you use them.

I notice several things about a bathroom when I see it for the first time. One glance around the room tells me a little about the

photo by Mary Nichols/design by Steve Chase & Associates

Beyond the balanced architecture of this man's dressing room lies asymmetrical space planning. I specified double-deep drawers and an under-sink pull-out tray. The far cabinet elegantly hides a TV.

client and a lot about how the space is currently being used. Here are some of the things I notice.

■ Is there space to put everything?

■ Are there wet towels hanging or piled on the floor?

■ Is there anything attractive or aesthetically detracting about the space?

■ Can two people walk around the room without bumping into one another?

■ Which way do the doors open?

■ Are there windows? Where are they located? Which way do they open?

■ Where are the fixtures in relation to one another?

■ Is there a dressing table or space for one?

■ Are there one or two sinks?

■ What's on the walls?

Observing the space is the first step in evaluating its potential. The next step is interviewing the owners to find out how well or how poorly the space now meets their needs.

Space planning a bathroom can be tricky. Because it is a limited space—and most people don't want to incur the expense of relocating plumbing lines—finding unused space is a challenge. But not an insurmountable one. Before I offer some ideas for organizing the bath, let me first tell you what's nonnegotiable. The following is what every well-planned bathroom should have.

■ Elbowroom at the sink

■ Room for another person to pass while you're standing at the sink

■ Concealed but convenient access to tub or shower plumbing

■ Hampers, wastebaskets

■ Mirrors that will allow you to see the back of your head or outfit

■ Magnifying mirrors for shaving and putting on makeup

■ Space for towels, paper products, robes

■ Space for storing toiletries and bathroom cleaning supplies

■ Space for small electronic items such as hair dryers (TVs and phones optional)

■ Sufficient outlets within view of a mirror but safely away from water sources

■ Space for medications that are taken in the morning or evening only. Pills that are taken throughout the day belong in the kitchen.

Making room for everything may mean structural changes, but not always and not always major ones. The best time to space plan a bathroom is when you're building or remodeling it. This is when you custom design or modify a pullman to fit your space and needs exactly. You can make the side-to-side dimensions of the cabinet under the sink smaller and the drawers wider. But if you don't have the luxury of fortuitous timing, then the following photos and drawings will show you some ways to gain storage and organize your bathroom.

© Michael Garland. Robbin Hayne. architect. Maxine Ordesky, space design. (both photos)

KIDS' BATHROOMS

Children play everywhere, including in the bath. I recall many a bath time when my own boys wouldn't even go near the tub unless their favorite floating toy was close at hand. But toys can be dangerous things in bathrooms if left lying around. So here's what you can do to make your child's bathroom fun, safe, and special.

■ Hang mirrors at eye level, as well as above the counter.

■ If a child shares your bathroom, give them their own drawer or shelf. This will keep their things where they belong and make it easier for you to maneuver around the space.

■ Be sure kids can reach what they need but not what they shouldn't.

■ Conceal a pull-out, pop-up step stool in a cabinet toe-kick.

■ Install safety latches on drawers or cabinets that hold medications.

■ Use only nonslip surfaces in tubs, showers, and on the floor.

■ Retailers offer many sturdy, inexpensive items for stowing bathroom toys.

Courtesy Lillian Vernon

■ Supply houses that serve elementary schools often have wonderful things for holding toys and organizing children's possessions.

Left and above left (two views): Space planning and architecture together synthesize this client's design aesthetic with storage needs. My favorite organizing tricks—custom-sized drawers and pull-out trays—work in the bath, too.

L-SHAPED PULLMAN

PLAN VIEW

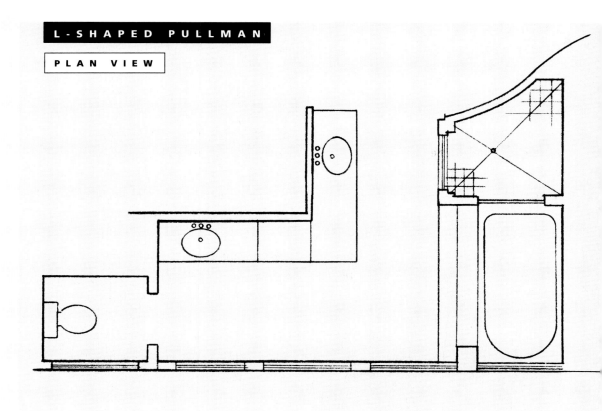

ELEVATED VIEW

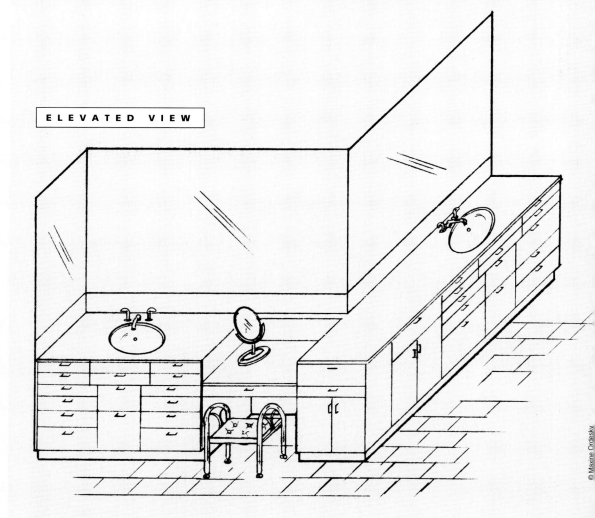

Right: The clients sharing this L-shaped room each desired their own space. This custom configuration of an L-shaped pullman works around the narrow room to offer personal counter space and substantial storage, even on the corner.

© Maxine Ordesky

FIGURING YOUR CONFIGURATION

Organizing your bathroom starts with space planning, and space planning starts with configuration. Bathrooms come in all shapes and sizes, just like the people who use them. Making the most of the shape of yours often means a little custom work. But in the long run, it's worth it. For instance, if your bathroom is long and narrow and the only pullman that will fit limits you to a tiny sink, install a custom unit that bulges out only around the sinks, similar to a baptismal font. This way you can get a bigger, more usable sink.

Conversely, if your bathroom is square or rectangular you could wrap, angle, or curve the pullmans around to fit the space. Utilizing corners is a good way to improve organization. With an L-shaped or curved pullman, you can separate the sinks for a semblance of privacy. Smooth, radiused edges are also safer in bathrooms.

Here's another bathroom myth down the you-know-what: The bathroom pullman can be any height you want it to be. Many taller clients wisely request pullmans that are higher than average to better accommodate their own height. Women may prefer to have a dressing-

© Michael Garland/Ronald McCoy, architect, Maxine Ordesky, space design

Courtesy Aristokraft

© Michael Garland/Ronald McCoy, architect, Maxine Ordesky, space design

Top left and left: A finished look at the bathroom shown opposite reveals the room's space planning and organization. Thirty-two drawers with inserts are designed specifically for this client's possessions and daily routine. Top right: Sloped platforms for cosmetics.

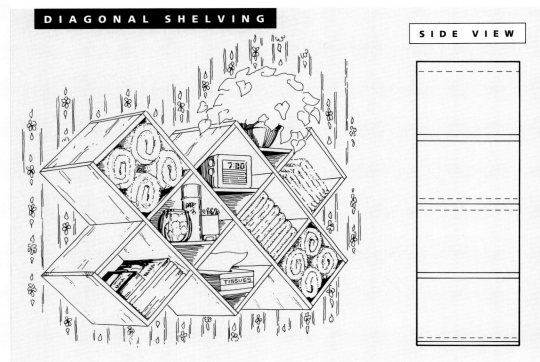

Top (both pages): This clever interlocking diagonal-shelving design is ideal bathroom storage. It's easily installed and built to hold any number of items, from towels to toiletries to tissues. I like it because there's a place for everything and everything is in its place. Plus, towels, or sweaters if you're hanging the unit inside a closet, won't topple over as they usually do when stacked on conventional shelves. The unit can be mounted anywhere and finished as you like it, assuming the finish weathers bathroom humidity. These drawings offer a good perspective for those who are construction-smart.

table section of a pullman measure as low as twenty-six or twenty-seven inches (66 or 68.5cm) high so that they can sit down to apply their makeup. The sink section, of course, is higher in these situations.

Who says the tub or pullman has to be against or between bathroom walls? Think unconventionally. Think island or peninsula when organizing a larger or odd-shaped room. In a large open bathroom, peninsulas work well to separate spaces and increase storage. Because peninsulas are anchored to a base wall, or a column in some cases, you can use that anchor to house recessed cabinets.

Bathroom space planning becomes particularly relevant in children's baths. Not only is safety a main concern, children often keep toys in the bathroom in addition to the toiletries that belong there! And, like adults, they want their bathrooms to be just for them. The sidebar on page 71 offers a few quick suggestions for space planning and organizing a child's bathroom. When space planning a child's bathroom, allow room for growth. Their needs and possessions will change—radically and rapidly!—as children become teenagers.

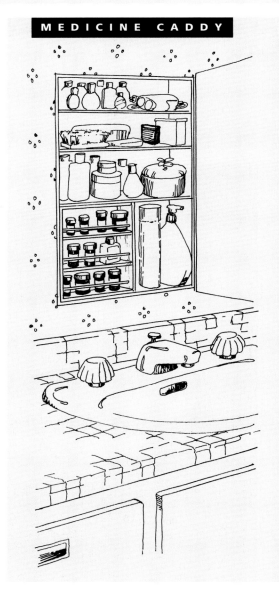

From 50 Storage Ideas For the Home by Kate Armpriester and Mary Jane Favorite (all illustrations)

FRONT VIEW

FRONT VIEW

SIDE VIEW

EXPLODED VIEW

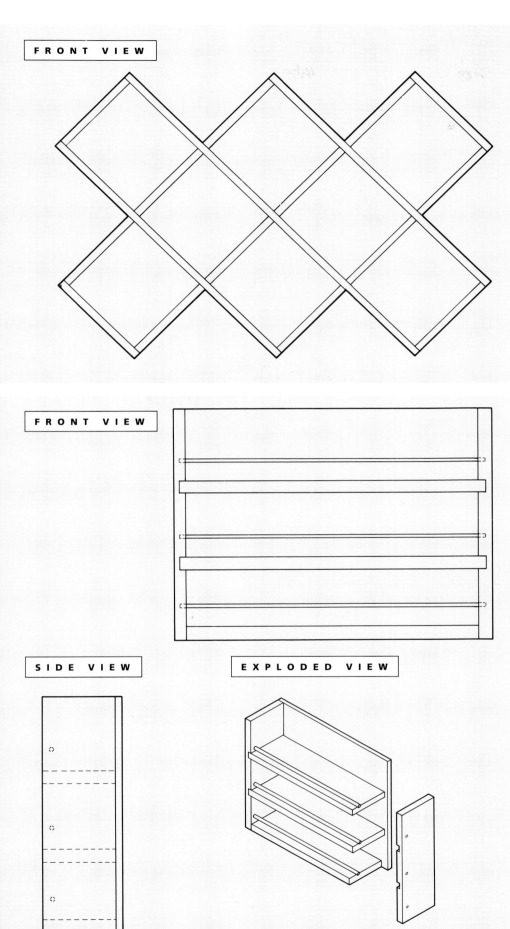

Bottom (both pages): Space planning and organizing the interior of a medicine cabinet is no different from organizing a closet or an entire room. Evaluate what you need to store and how you'll be retrieving those items. This space-making idea for retrofitting medicine cabinets essentially creates a smaller cabinet within the space, much like on-door spice bins do in the kitchen pantry. Build the custom insert shown here or purchase retail partitions. If you don't have a medicine cabinet, you can sometimes recess shelves into a bathroom wall as long as it contains no plumbing or electrical work. Voilà! You have a four-inch (10.1cm) -deep traditional-looking medicine cabinet.

BELOW-THE-SEAT HAMPER

ELEVATION

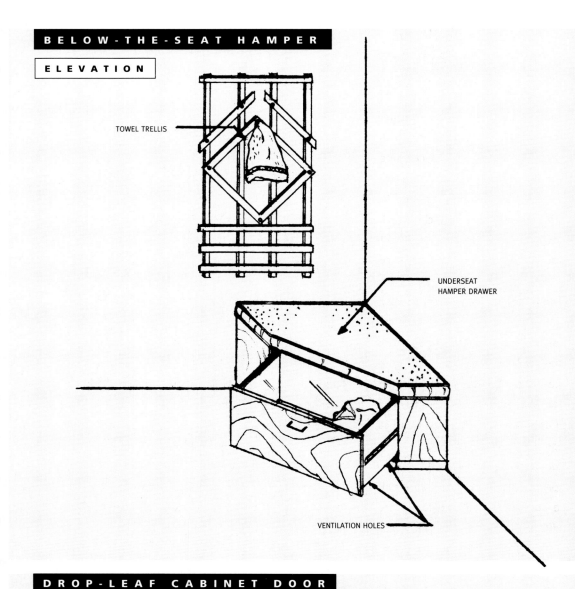

TOWEL TRELLIS

UNDERSEAT
HAMPER DRAWER

VENTILATION HOLES

Above right: Every bathroom has at least one place to sit down, but when space planning bathrooms, especially new constructions, I like to add a second with a pull-out hamper. Ventilate hampers with small air holes. Right: Like a secretary-style desk, a drop-leaf door on a bathroom cabinet provides an extra work surface when open and private storage when closed. I used this trick in my own bathroom—and in clients'. This is space planning at its best.

DROP-LEAF CABINET DOOR

ELEVATION

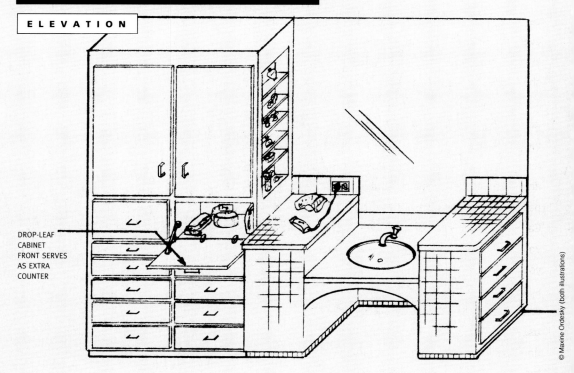

DROP-LEAF
CABINET
FRONT SERVES
AS EXTRA
COUNTER

© Maxine Ordesky (both illustrations)

POWDER ROOMS

Advice on space planning and organizing bathrooms would be incomplete without a nod toward powder rooms. To me, a true powder room—a room frequented *only* by company—is the consummate luxury. Not to have to scurry around cleaning a bathroom before guests arrive and being able to store nothing but pretty soaps and hand towels in the drawers would be close to heaven for my compulsive, obsessive personality! But since I don't have such a space, I live vicariously through my clients. Let's talk a moment about ways to organize powder rooms.

Naturally, the drawers and shelves can hold all sorts of things besides soaps and towels. Realize, however, that guests do peek. In fact, a recent study revealed that 97 percent of those questioned admitted to looking through other people's bathroom drawers and cabinets. If your powder room is sufficiently large and you're desperate for extra space, you could section off part of the room behind a door. Behind it place a custom- or ready-made storage unit to hold linens, books, games, coats, almost anything.

A powder room can even double as a laundry room, assuming there's room to conceal a stacked washer/dryer unit behind louvered doors, for example. Maybe you could even borrow a few feet from the powder room in order to make room for full-size appliances, shelves, or other laundry room storage.

At the opposite end of my powder-bath fantasy is having one that I don't need! If you're lucky enough to be in this situation, I suggest removing the fixtures, shutting off the plumbing, and making the space a storage room. Or a pantry. Or a small office. Or any room you need. Carefully wrap and package the fixtures, and you'll be able to use them again someday if your space needs shift back the other way. This suggestion holds true for his and her bathrooms or two-sink pullmans if only one person actually uses the bathroom. Remove the fixtures you don't need, disconnect the plumbing, and utilize the space for something you do need.

Top: Originally, this small guest bath had a pedestal sink. The client wanted more storage and room to maneuver; this angled pullman achieves both. Left and above (two views): A two-part cabinet designed specifically as back-wall (above-the-W.C.) storage.

CHAPTER FOUR

BEDROOMS

Left: Old-fashioned steamer trunks are a charming way to store seasonal bedding in the bedroom. Above (two views): These custom bedside secretaries, which I designed for a client's New York apartment, have dropleaf writing surfaces and drawers sized to hold small items such as gloves, socks, and lingerie.

Bedrooms are to the home what the easy chair is to the end of a hard day. The private refuge where we retreat to relax and rejuvenate, bedrooms are sanctuaries that fulfill a variety of emotional, psychological, and physical needs. We wind down—and up—in our bedrooms. We hide there. We dream, occasionally scheme, and of course, we sleep in these rooms.

For many of us, the bedroom is guardian of our most precious memories: pictures of our children and pictures of ourselves when we were our children's ages. For children, bedrooms are their very own worlds, their primary play area and learning center. Space planning and organizing such sacrosanct rooms seems almost blasphemous. The truth is, however, that good space planning will enhance a bedroom just as it will every other room of the house.

The bedroom as adult sanctuary should be comfortable and welcoming; as a child's very special place of his or her own, the bedroom should be capable of handling all the clutter and action his or her imagination can realize. And it should adapt as the child grows.

Space planning is the means to both ends.

At first glance, bedrooms don't seem all that complex, at least not in comparison to kitchens or bathrooms. So how do you know when your bedroom needs space planning? Well, start by reading the following statements. Do any of them apply to you?

■ Your route to the closet or bathroom is circuitous.

■ You have to circumnavigate the bed to reach the dresser, door, or closet.

■ You're reading by flashlight.

■ You bring a glass of water to bed at night but have to put it on the floor.

■ You can't use the room the way you wish.

■ You no longer delight in your bedroom as a refuge.

■ You have to move something aside or contort yourself just to open a drawer.

■ Stacks of magazines, books, or shoes obscure your baseboards.

■ You're always bumping into furniture.

■ Your carpet is wearing your wardrobe.

■ You get one side of the bed and your clutter gets the other.

SPACE PLANNING
A CHILD'S ROOM

Divide and conquer. That's the best strategy for organizing a child's room. Provide your child with enough containers of all sizes and shapes to sufficiently hold their various belongings: one for the baseball cards, another for the rock collection. Keep toys and games separate from Legos and reading material. Also try these ideas.

■ Utilize horizontal planes—build out and across rather than up—until they grow tall enough to reach high bookcases and shelves. Hang mirrors at their eye level.

■ Use a headboard or bookcases to partition the room into activity centers.

■ Allow plenty of floor space for playing. Buy or build bunk beds; elevate a single bed on a platform or loft so floor space remains available.

■ Place bed in a natural niche or alcove to maximize floor space.

■ Buy a chest or use a footlocker to store awkward-sized and odd-shaped toys. These storage items do double duty when the time comes to pack your child for camp and college.

■ Plan organized storage for "leave-out" toys versus "put-away" toys. Puzzles in progress, for example, could be left on a table that can be covered with a custom-made lid. This lid fits neatly over the puzzle pieces and provides ample work surface for another project.

■ Wheeled storage works well in a child's room. Rolling chests can glide under the bed or zoom into the closet; rolling toy carts are great because your child can pull the empty chest to his or her toys, clean up, and pull the full container back to its dock.

Top: This all-in-one arrangement for a child's room has space for storage, sleeping, and playing. Bottom: Colorful retail bins are organizing wizards in children's rooms.

Interior Design: Susan Fredman - Interior Accents, Highland Park, Il/Photo: Ellis of Jessie Walker & Associates

Courtesy Lillian Vernon

Get the picture? Essentially, when the room doesn't work for you or for your child, it's time to space plan. Actually, with respect to children's rooms, it's always time to space plan. Begin organizing a child's room from the word "Congratulations!" Buy infant furniture that will grow into the toddler years at least and beyond at best. Trust me: Before you even learn how to spell bassinet, you'll be buying a computer.

Children of all ages store books, games, toys, stuffed animals, and clothes in their bedrooms. Today, electronics and telephones seem to pop up earlier and earlier. Children's activities also require all sorts of paraphernalia, so space planning and storage in children's rooms should be activity related. These photographs present some ideas, and the sidebar on this page takes a quick look at a few others.

So you see, the trick to space planning a child's room is once again flexibility, reachability, and perspective—theirs, not yours. Involve your child in organizing his or her room so they'll feel a part of it and, hopefully, be more inclined to keep it organized. Children's rooms are generally way too small to be all the things they need to be. Space planning the room, carefully choosing the correct size, shape, and type of furnishings, will help keep the room shipshape over the years. The same goes for you, too, Mom and Dad.

An adult's bedroom may appear more stagnant than a child's, but it's really not. Grown-ups do more than sleep in their rooms. Some people virtually live in their bedrooms, surrounding themselves with their TVs, stereos, VCRs, computers, desks, bills, reading, and so on. Bedrooms are also, much to our chagrin, catchalls for anything we don't want company to see but haven't found the time or space to store elsewhere. And because bedrooms aren't really public rooms, we often clutter them with the items we don't want lying around.

But a cluttered bedroom isn't what I'd call romantic. Quite the opposite, unless of

course you like it that way—and some people do. If you're such a person, please don't take offense to the advice that follows. Maybe you should skip to a different chapter. For those who aren't so fond of clutter in the bedroom, the sidebar on this page will help you evaluate your space-planning needs.

Furniture placement is central to good space planning. In a bedroom, the bed is generally the largest and most cumbersome piece of furniture. Most rooms have an obvious spot for a bed but few take into account traffic flow through the room. If possible, and if it complements the view from your bedroom windows, place your bed wherever it's the least intrusive; that way you'll salvage more usable floor space and avoid circumnavigating the bed every time you want to get to the other side of the room. Conventional beds can be placed on platforms, custom or ready-made, which in turn provide excellent storage space. But keep the room's proportions in mind. An elevated bed may not look good beneath a low ceiling. The room might feel too condensed.

SPACE PLANNING
THE BEDROOM

Before overhauling your room and charging into a local furniture store, ask yourself a few questions about how you use your bedroom. Just like kitchen or bathroom space planning, it's helpful to understand your habits before adapting the space to complement those routines.

[1] How many people get dressed there? What is each person's morning and evening routine?

[2] Do you have any special needs relevant to dressing for social or business occasions?

[3] How often do you pack for trips in your bedroom?

[4] What else do you want to do in your bedroom? Sewing? Reading? Office or home paperwork?

[5] Do you wish to hang art on the walls? Display photos on furniture or walls?

[6] Do you prefer to keep your bedroom door open or closed?

[7] Do you have any different habits on weekends that should be accommodated?

[8] Do you watch TV in the bedroom? Or listen to music?

[9] Is your closet space sufficient or do you need more clothes storage in your bedroom?

[10] Where do you put extra bed linens at night?

[11] Do you exercise in your bedroom?

Above left: Placing trim directly on drawers rather than in between expands each drawer to its maximum capacity. Left: Building out the cabinets in this bedroom sitting area created a cozy window alcove as well as counter and cabinet storage.

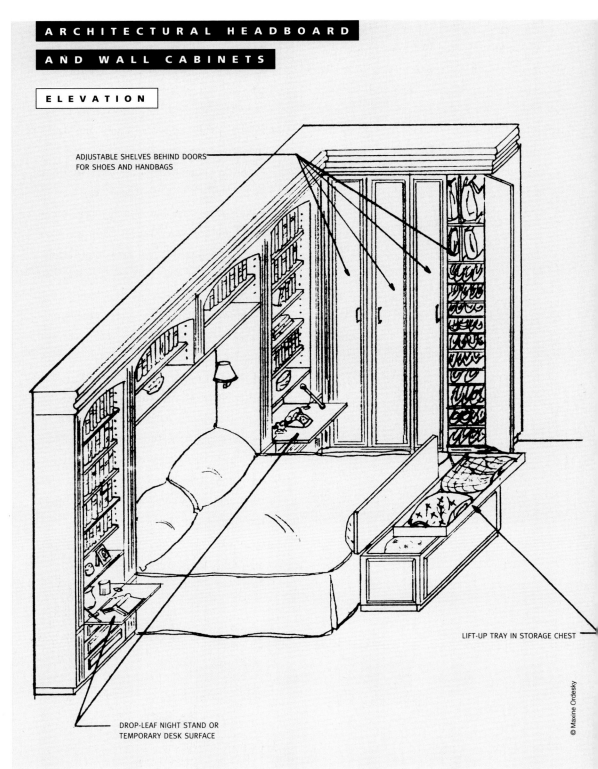

ARCHITECTURAL HEADBOARD AND WALL CABINETS

ELEVATION

ADJUSTABLE SHELVES BEHIND DOORS
FOR SHOES AND HANDBAGS

LIFT-UP TRAY IN STORAGE CHEST

DROP-LEAF NIGHT STAND OR
TEMPORARY DESK SURFACE

© Maxine Ordesky

This drawing shows yet another view of the bedroom pictured on the previous page. The architectural millwork surrounding the room cloaks gorgeous closets that are space planned to the last inch, including toe-in/toe-out shoe storage.

Other than the bed, bedrooms typically contain a bureau and/or a chest of drawers, nightstands, and with any luck, an audio/video cabinet. Larger bedrooms may also include a seating area. More and more, however, drawer units are finding their way into closets as a means of freeing up bedroom floor space. No bedroom, as far as I'm concerned, is complete without a nightstand on either side of

the bed and some sort of storage at the foot of the bed: a chest, a dresser, even a stylish bench with a lift-up seat. Where else in the house is it permissible and desirable to so closely surround a piece of furniture with other functional pieces? If you don't have at least two nightstands, you're indeed ignoring potential bedroom storage space.

Other hot spots for bedroom storage space

are under windows, on wall returns, and within freestanding pieces such as trunks. Just as in the dining room, window seats and shallow shelves built into walls between the studs make excellent places for storage. Custom headboards can incorporate nightstands. Cabinets—custom made or store-bought—positioned at the foot of the bed can hold televisions (high-tech cabinets offer pop-up mechanisms for TV storage) and generate additional storage space in the bedroom.

If you're looking for a bigger bedroom without adding on, check your local building codes to see about enclosing a balcony or porch. (This is a much more feasible construction project if your home's roof line already extends over the chosen space.) Or turn an enclosed balcony into a closet—you already have a doorway—and expand the bedroom into the existing closet. Going the other way, you could also sacrifice two feet (0.6m) of bedroom floor space to

enlarge your closet. If you make the closet large enough for a center island or peninsula (see the chapter on closets), you may not need chests in your bedroom. That would certainly open up the room's sleeping area.

And what about fireplaces? If you're lucky enough to have a fireplace in your bedroom, you'll probably want to keep it as such. But if it's a nonworking unit or you could do without it, turn the space into bookshelves, cabinets, drawers, an entertainment center, you name it. Either way, it's found storage space that will help you in organizing your bedroom.

A final note: When buying bedroom furniture, for adults or children, buy storage-intensive pieces. That way you can buy fewer. Your sanctuary will remain as is, without clutter or big awkward furniture. Don't forget either that an armoire with cleverly arranged, custom-planned shelves and interior spaces can hold a TV, books, bed linens, and even lighting.

Top (left and right): In this client's New York bedroom, a custom dresser with acrylic drawer inserts and pull-out palettes makes the most of available space. Above: Cherry wood adds a romantic touch.

CHAPTER FIVE

CLOSETS

© Michael Garland/Maxine Ordesky, space design

© Phillip H. Ennis

Your closet is your personal boutique, sumptuously and efficiently displaying your wardrobe. Left: A man's custom wall closet takes full advantage of vertical space and doors. Right: This client and her husband share a large walk-in closet with a dividing peninsula for packing and meticulously planned storage for clothes, shoes, and accessories.

If you promise not to laugh, I'll tell you a secret. I used to dream about closets. It's true. Many years ago, before I started my space-planning business, I dreamed about the world's most perfect closet.

On more than one occasion, I dreamed I heard industrious noises coming from my tiny wall closet. As I opened the door to investigate, I saw a troupe of gnomes busily sewing on loose buttons, tacking hemlines, dutifully ironing, and carefully removing telltale spots from my clothes. Everything was in perfect

repair, securely hung from the right hanger, and so organized! While this may seem like a strange dream, it was most inspiring to me.

Needless to say, my passion for organization and well-used space had crept into my sleeping hours. With four people—including two toddlers—living in a small rented home, my own closet was really the only space in the entire house I could keep under control and organized. I converted that wall closet into a small but glorious walk-in closet and just kept going from there. In my next life, I'll have a closet so large that I can get dressed in it without leaving—everything I need will be at hand. Every shoe, handbag, belt, scarf, and accessory will have a home of its own. Hanging garments will be separated just enough so that nothing will touch—no wrinkles. My dream closet will have a transit lounge—a designated spot to temporarily keep items destined for the dry cleaners, tailors, or a local charity. My own personal boutique...

Of course there is no such thing as the ideal closet. Closets are as individual as the people whose belongings they hold. However, there is such a thing as a closet with the right features for you. To get that closet of your dreams, my first piece of advice is to consider hiring a professional space planner, especially if your home is in the construction or remodeling phase. If that's not a viable option, then

follow the usual strategy. Evaluate your needs and life-style (see the sidebar on the opposite page), and measure them against your existing closet space. First, you'll have to accept some general ailments that often afflict closets.

The Grand Central Station of the home, closets are often the place of choice for hiding heating and air-conditioning equipment, duct work, telephone and alarm equipment, and plumbing access panels. Fortunately, there are space-planning solutions for working around such impediments, as you'll see in some of the illustrations on the following pages. Be prepared, too, for gender differences. The configuration—anatomy, if you will—is different. At the risk of generalizing, men's closets are typically less complex than women's. Despite men's newfound passion for fashion, women's wardrobes and clothing needs remain more

Courtesy Maxine Ordesky

Above: This elegant armoire wall, as I like to call it, extends to the bathroom pullman in this client's dressing room. Right: The slightly bumped-out center section allows just enough room for on-door tie dowels. Hanging poles are adjustable.

Courtesy Maxine Ordesky

involved and varied than men's. Naturally, there are exceptions for both sexes, but for the most part, this difference holds true. You'll see what I mean as you read how to space plan a man's closet versus that of a woman's. Before moving into these differences, however, it's important to consider structural distinctions between the most common types of clothing closets—wall, walk-in, and step-in.

WHAT IS YOUR CLOSET TYPE?

Closets are generally of the wall or walk-in variety. Between these standards, I add my own classification of step-in. Such closets are just deep and wide enough for you to stand inside and turn around 360 degrees. Personally and professionally, I prefer walk-in closets whenever possible, but wall closets do have their champions.

Wall closets, which typically measure approximately twenty-four inches (60.9cm) deep, do not consume floor space to the extent that walk-ins do, which makes them more economical in very space-tight homes. For the same reason, they're also an efficient way to add closet space to a room where none exists. Functionally, wall closets are best reserved as coat closets, guest room closets, or secondary and seasonal storage. Wall closets would be more universally useful if they were a little deeper and had better lighting so you could more clearly see into the far ends and above the door.

The disadvantages of wall closets are— sadly—numerous. Perhaps the greatest restriction is that the standard door and interior configurations make it difficult to see the closet's entire contents at the same time. In wall closets, space is often lost at either end of the stretch where there is wall instead of doorway. You can't see into this area or get things in and out without manipulating clothing. Finally, wall closets with folding or sliding doors really don't have anywhere to hang belts and ties. Yes, you can buy special racks to hang on the pole, but

once you load these items, they generally become too awkward to use. Besides, they use up precious hanging space on the pole. Having said all this, it becomes clear that most people are living with less-than-adequate wall closets. Hang on. There are things you can do to alleviate the crunch.

The first option is to use the existing closet to its potential. It's been my experience that a man's or child's wardrobe fits better into a wall closet than does a woman's. Her varied needs are better suited to a walk-in design. You should also plan the best way to utilize side returns and backs of doors. In fact, you may even consider changing your doors to improve access into the entire closet. You should also replace the standard pole and shelf system with a series of adjustable shelves and poles (see Tricks of the Trade in Part I, Chapter 4).

© Michael Garland/Maxine Ordesky, space design

Use pull-outs if you can, and designate separate areas for shelving and double-hanging of shorter items. Never, never, never put existing dressers or chests of drawers into wall closets. It's okay to custom-build drawer units that work in harmony with the limited confines of a wall closet. If you're really desperate and ambitious and your wall closet measures at least four by six feet (1.21 by 1.8m), trick it into believing it's a walk-in closet. The before-and-after drawing on the next page shows how I deceived my own

A small section of compartmentalized pull-out trays built into a wall closet gives this client a staging area and room to display her favorite photos. Trays hold the accessories for the garments that hang in the surrounding closet.

CONVERTING A WALL CLOSET INTO A WALK-IN

BEFORE

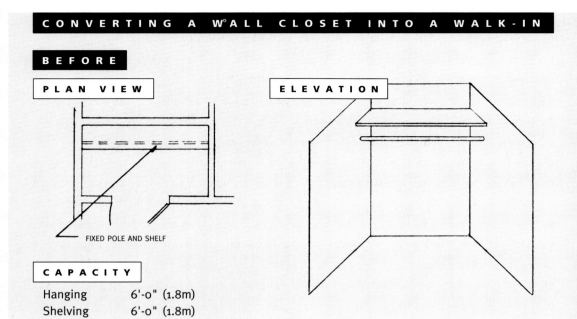

PLAN VIEW

FIXED POLE AND SHELF

ELEVATION

CAPACITY

Hanging   6'-0" (1.8m)
Shelving   6'-0" (1.8m)

AFTER

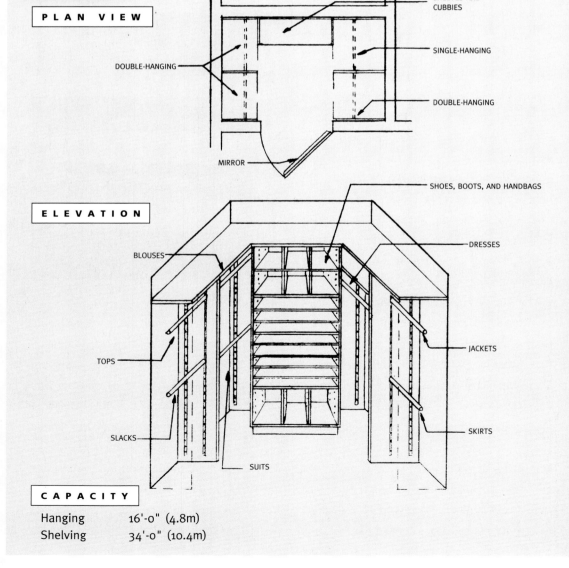

PLAN VIEW

DOUBLE-HANGING

SHELVES AND CUBBIES

SINGLE-HANGING

DOUBLE-HANGING

MIRROR

ELEVATION

SHOES, BOOTS, AND HANDBAGS

BLOUSES

DRESSES

TOPS

JACKETS

SLACKS

SKIRTS

SUITS

CAPACITY

Hanging   16'-0" (4.8m)
Shelving   34'-0" (10.4m)

Space planning can trick a deep wall closet into acting like a small walk-in. My own closet gained an additional ten feet (3m) for a total of sixteen feet (4.8m) of hanging space, eight shoe shelves, six handbag cubbies, three boot cubbies, and a luggage shelf. I practice what I preach!

wall closet. You might also consider adding a freestanding piece to hold those items that can't be properly accommodated in your wall closet.

Now let's talk about walk-in closets. There's so much I could say; they're a space planner's dream come true, especially a space planner who's as closet crazy as I am! The most innovative, problem-solving designs for disorganized closets can be put to the test in walk-ins. The larger the walk-in, the more flexible, adaptable, and personal the finished closet. The options are endless. I've designed walk-in closets as large as rooms. They can have everything from running water to small refrigerators to revolving shelves. Ironing boards, steamers, shoe-polishing kits and seats, dressing tables with lighted mirrors, islands, and peninsulas are all standard fare in many walk-in closets. I could gush on and on about walk-ins, but lest you think I've lost all objectivity, let me point out their disadvantages as well.

To get the most from a walk-in closet, the space should measure at least ten feet (3m) wide. Consequently, walk-ins can usurp floor space from other rooms. Lighting may not always be sufficient, either. But these deterrents are merely factors to incorporate into the design concept. They're not significant impediments to an organized, efficient closet.

SHARE AND SHARE ALIKE

All is not equal when it comes to sharing closet space. When a husband and wife share a closet, 98 percent of the time she has more space than he does. Usually it's because she has a more varied wardrobe. The best way to organize a shared closet is to maintain a friendly distance. You've heard the saying that fences make good neighbors? Well, so do separate drawers and shelves. Organize a shared closet so that his space is separate from hers. In walk-in closets, a peninsula or island is a good way to do this congenially. A little separation will help you each find what you need faster and improve the traffic flow. You won't be crisscrossing each other's paths to reach for your clothes as you dress.

The other trick to space planning a shared closet is taking into account personal differences such as height or reach. If the man can outreach the woman, his clothes can hang higher to take full advantage of all the

HOW HIGH IS TOO HIGH?

To establish your maximum comfortable reach, follow these steps. First, stand as far away from a wall as you normally stand from your closet poles or shelves, probably about ten inches (2.3cm). Next, extend your arm, marking the spot where your hand touches the wall. That distance is your guide for space planning your closet. Keep in mind that you can reach approximately six inches (15.2cm) higher with a hanger in your hand than you can with a folded garment. Knowing this, I advise my clients to store extra hangers on a short closet pole placed above their hanging garments.

The clients who share this closet travel often and prefer hanging to folding. To suit their life-style, I designed a peninsula with pull-out hanging space and pull-out palettes on the back wall to hold sweaters and hats.

TEN COMMANDMENTS (+1) OF ORGANIZED CLOSETS

If there was a skeleton in your closet could you find it? No closet is too big or too small to organize. While not carved in stone, these "commandments" will help improve closets of all shapes, sizes, and disorder. The objective is to make all vertical and horizontal space in your closet usable without limiting accessibility or visibility.

1. Thou shalt put nothing on thy floor.
2. Thou shalt hang garments as close to thy floor as possible.
3. Thou shalt double-hang short items.
4. Thou shalt place single-hanging items at eye level with more shelving above.
5. Thou shalt make all shelves and poles adjustable.
6. Thou shalt maintain a separate section of shelving.
7. Thou shalt install pull-outs wherever possible.
8. Thou shalt buy and use correct hangers for thy garments.
9. Thou shalt not hang empty hangers among thy clothing.
10. Thou shalt hang garments so that each item faces thee.
11. Thou shalt return all dry cleaner's hangers to thy dry cleaner.

© Michael Garland/Maxine Ordesky, space design

Above right: Short garments should double-hang, grouped by category when possible and always within reach. Right: I specify pull-out hanging for clients who have sufficient room in their closet for an island or peninsula and don't need drawers.

closet space. Similarly, if the majority of his clothes are short enough to be double-hung, they should be, leaving room for both of their longer garments. Of course, if you're planning to build a custom shared closet, you can make it as personal as two individual closets.

ISLANDS AND PENINSULAS

A walk-in closet without an island or peninsula is not complete. What these storage gems add to the kitchen, they can also bring to the closet. Islands are terrific places to introduce flat packing or folding surfaces and have drawers or pull-out palettes. They're also diplomatic dividing lines between his and her items or different clothing categories, because they still facilitate conversation between the closet users.

© Michael Garland/Maxine Ordesky, space design

MEN'S CLOSETS

Once upon a time not so many years ago, there lived an average man named Joe Wardrobe. For an average man, Joe had an average closet. He owned approximately three or four suits; three jackets; six pairs of slacks; six pairs of jeans, khakis, and corduroys; a dozen shirts; three sweaters; eighteen T-shirts; a few pairs of shoes; three or four belts; and ten or twelve ties, which he had received as birthday and holiday gifts. Joe's closet was easy to keep organized. Most of his things were roughly the same size and took up about the same amount of space in the closet. Joe's friends had similar, average closets. Sure, some friends had life-styles or careers that required more extensive wardrobes and still others needed only one suit and a few more leisure clothes, but mostly they were the same.

Then one day, Joe Wardrobe went to the mall. He saw many, many stores that sold nothing but men's clothes. Some sold only ties! He saw cosmetic counter after cosmetic counter displaying men's toiletries. Joe was overcome with individuality and choice. He acquired his own style, his own scent, even his own personalized skin treatment. Joe Wardrobe's wardrobe exploded. His toiletries grew by leaps and bounds. But his closet remained its average size. Where did he put it all?

The onset of men's heightened interest in fashion and grooming was considerably more gradual than Joe's. However, it is only within the last decade that the variety and complexity of men's clothes and toiletries has come close to matching that of women's. The more items men crammed into their closets, the more frustrating it became to get dressed in the morning. So how does our tale end? With a very organized closet.

INSIDE THE MAN'S CLOSET

There's more to a man's ensemble than meets the eye. How many items can you name?
- Suits and tuxedos
- Sport jackets
- Dress slacks
- Jeans and casual slacks
- Shirts (dress, casual, knit, and T-shirts)
- Outerwear jackets and coats
- Footwear (dress shoes, casual shoes, athletic shoes, boots, slippers)
- Ties
- Belts and suspenders
- Hats, gloves, scarves
- Briefcases and overnight bags
- Exercise clothing and equipment
- Handkerchiefs
- Bathrobes
- Underwear, undershirts, and socks
- Cuff links, jewelry, watches
- Tie clips, collar stays
- Tuxedo accessories

© Michael Garland/Maxine Ordesky, space design

I planned the man's side of this shared closet to accommodate his preference for hanging pants long, which meant starting shoe shelves right above the hanging space and storing ties on dowels in a custom pull-out cabinet next to his shirts.

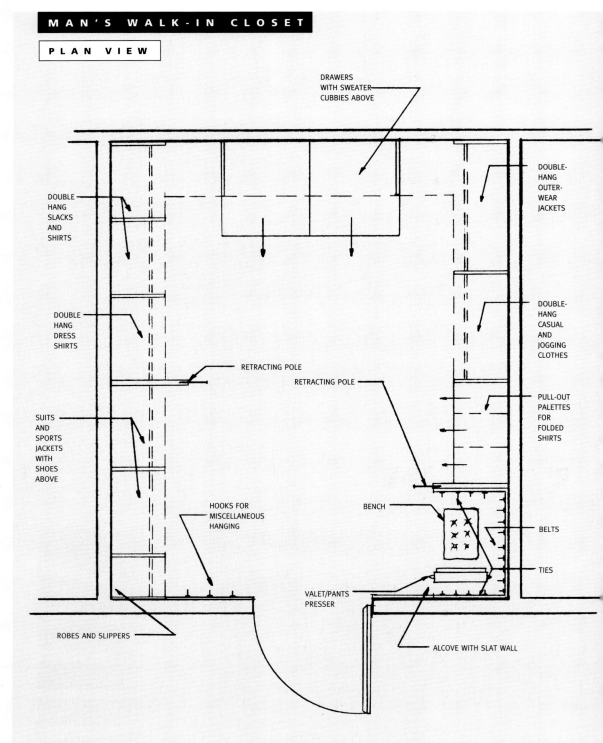

MAN'S WALK-IN CLOSET

PLAN VIEW

DRAWERS WITH SWEATER CUBBIES ABOVE

DOUBLE HANG SLACKS AND SHIRTS

DOUBLE HANG DRESS SHIRTS

RETRACTING POLE

RETRACTING POLE

SUITS AND SPORTS JACKETS WITH SHOES ABOVE

HOOKS FOR MISCELLANEOUS HANGING

BENCH

DOUBLE-HANG OUTER-WEAR JACKETS

DOUBLE-HANG CASUAL AND JOGGING CLOTHES

PULL-OUT PALETTES FOR FOLDED SHIRTS

BELTS

TIES

VALET/PANTS PRESSER

ROBES AND SLIPPERS

ALCOVE WITH SLAT WALL

In this client's large walk-in closet, slat wall with movable hat hooks lines an alcove furnished with a chair and valet/pants presser. Belts and ties are adjacent; clothing hangs categorically; tennis attire and gear are all in one place.

CAPACITY

Suits	4'-0" (1.2m)		Casual and jogging	4'-0" (1.2m)
Slacks	3'-0" (.91m)		Shoes	46 pairs
Shirts	4'-0" (1.2m)		Drawers	12
Jackets	6'-0" (1.8m)		Palettes	36

WHAT MEN WANT FROM THEIR CLOSETS

Organizing a closet is not high on most men's list of priorities. Men are what I term "closet" closet organizers. They're hesitant at first, but once they see the benefits, they embrace the idea wholeheartedly. Besides, it's easier to group men's clothes because there is less variation in a man's wardrobe.

A man's idea of an organized closet is an easy closet. They like to hook and toss things rather than fuss with a hanger. Nor do they take the time to carefully fold and stack sweaters. They do like an area to coordinate suits, shirts, and ties. Men also like gadgets and mechanisms. Many men ask for swing-down footrests or folding seats so they don't have to leave their closet to put on shoes and socks. They don't want to move three belts or five ties to reach the one they want.

A man's closet must be functional, and keep in mind that they don't have much enthusiasm for arranging their clothes or maintaining their closets. But running counter to all this is the fact that many men are indeed very particular about how their clothes are stored...if asked. Some insist on storing all their shirts folded while others will only hang them. This is in fact related to how they like their shirts laundered and—for frequent travelers—what type of suitcase they use when traveling. Many men hang all their shirts, even T-shirts and knit sport shirts. Some men refuse to fold pants over a hanger, preferring (as do I if space allows) to hang them long. I've even had male clients tell me they don't want to lift one sweater to get at another.

WHAT WOMEN WANT FROM MEN'S CLOSETS

The first thing women want from a man's closet is separation. Which works out fine, because most men prefer not sharing a closet with the women in their lives, either. My

Spatially, closets are the home's unsung heroes. Only of late are architects and builders paying more attention to closet design. Unfortunately, most closets are not planned with an eye toward the future. Making room for what you own is only half the battle in planning your closet. The other half is allowing for growth. If you're on the brink of a career or life-style change, you may be able to anticipate what types of clothes you'll be acquiring or eliminating in the future. The trick to wholly organizing your closet is anticipating future needs and making your closet adjustable enough to accommodate change without requiring new construction.

Study your own clothing categories and buying habits, noting which clothes you buy most often and how much space you think new purchases will require. As you allot hanging space in your closet, allocate extra space for items in proportion to your habits and needs. If you own twice as many blouses and suits as anything else, it's likely you'll need 50 percent more of your space for new blouses and suits.

One way to deter your closet from rebelling over the long term is to a keep a container in it; even a shopping bag or laundry basket will work. Whenever you put on something that you don't like or vow you'll never wear again, take it off and put it in that bag. Don't hang the garment back up. When your container fills, donate the clothes.

HOW MUCH IS ENOUGH?

Once you know how much space each type of clothing requires, you can better space plan your closet to fit your wardrobe. When hung, the following men's apparel take up approximately the noted inches (or centimeters). The type of hanger you use and the thickness of the material may add or detract from the measurements shown below. Looking at a pair of man's slacks hanging long or folded, they only need sixteen or seventeen inches (40.6 to 43.1cm) of depth in the closet. Suits, shirts, and jackets require twenty-two inches (55.8cm) of depth. Hence, a narrow place (usually where you first enter the closet or at the side returns in a wall closet) would be a good place to put slacks. Please note: Actual dimensions may vary with different clothing sizes.

ITEM	LENGTH (from top of hanger hook to bottom of garment)	THICKNESS (each garment including hanger)
Suit	38"–42" (96.5–106.6cm)	3" (7.6cm) or more
Dress shirt	38"–42" (96.5–106.6cm)	1/2" (1.2cm) or less; 1/4" (0.6cm) if on a wire hanger
Polo/sport shirt	38"–42" (96.5–106.6cm)	1/2" (1.2cm) or less
Folded slacks	28"–32" (71.1–81.2cm)	1/2–3/4" (1.9–2.5cm)
Long-hanging slacks	48"–54" (121.9–137.1cm)	3/4"–1" (1.9cm)
Ties	30"–33" (76.2–83.8cm)	same width as the tie
Dress belts	38"–44" (96.5–111.7cm)	1"–1 1/2" (2.5–3.8cm)

Men's wardrobes are usually not complex. This client's closet was easily organized behind two sets of center-opening doors. Business and dress garments comprise one half, casual clothes the other. And it's all adjustable!

women clients express high hopes that having an organized closet of their own will discourage their husbands from spilling their pocket contents on any old desktop. Face it, guys. You start putting things in your pockets as soon as you learn how. Pens, loose change, breath mints, and paper scraps are merely the grown-up version of seashells, baseball cards, and gum wrappers.

The daily pocket emptying is a sacred ritual, so treat it as such. Plan a staging area, a spot where you can sort through your pocket's contents at day's end and dispose of things accordingly. Partition a drawer with

custom-made or store-bought inserts sized to hold whatever your pockets do. You'll be surprised how such a little step can lead to bigger and better organizing habits.

ORGANIZING A MAN'S CLOSET

Now we come to the nitty-gritty. The pictures in this section speak thousands of words. Fortunately, most things in a man's wardrobe can be double-hung, which immediately increases storage capacity twofold. Another quick fix is getting rid of what you don't need or wear. Some men insist that ties always come back in style and that someday they'll fit into that jacket again. If you aren't wearing it but can't part with it, at least get it out of the active closet and into a storage area. The only clothes or accessories that belong in closets—both men's and women's—are those that you enjoy wearing.

Decide which items you want to hang and which can be folded. Reposition your clothes in a logical manner that complements your life-style and wardrobe. Pick everything up off the floor and utilize high shelves for tall items such as boots, briefcases, or luggage. Categorizing men's clothes is sometimes the only way to accommodate quick and easy access. Because men's clothing is generally cut the same, it's easy to put them into sections but hard to differentiate between them. (A man's suit jacket is a suit jacket is a suit jacket. A woman's suit jacket might be one of three or four lengths and have a variety of collar styles.) Finally, buy the right hanger for each type of clothing.

SHOES AND SOCKS

Men don't usually have extensive shoe collections, but the shoes they do own often look similar. Men's dress shoes come in only so many styles, whereas women's dress shoes....The best way to store and organize men's shoes depends upon the type of space you have at your disposal. Slanted shoe shelves make it easy to distinguish each pair from the other since you can see most of the shoe.

As a space planner, my objection to slanted shelves is that they waste vertical space in the closet. So if space is an issue, men's shoes should be stored on flat shelves. In this arrangement, try to keep the shelves at eye level; above eye level, place the shoes with the heels facing toward you. You can see more of the shoe this way. Cowboy or ski boots should be positioned upright on the highest shelf in your closet. This is a good way to utilize your closet's full ceiling height.

As long as you can reach the bottom of the boot, the shelf isn't too high. Socks should be stored folded neatly in drawers, preferably in drawers that have been fitted with inserts to help organize the socks by color. I often try to build the sock drawer near the man's shoe shelf so he can easily and quickly match socks to his outfit.

SWEATERS AND FOLDED GARMENTS

Newton was definitely onto something when he discovered gravity. What's true about apples is equally true about stacks of sweaters: What goes up must come down. In the interest of organizing, I beg you, never stack folded items more than two or three garments high. A stack of eight or nine sweaters never gets restacked. Use pull-out trays or palettes in a one-to-one or, at the most, a one-to-three ratio. (You can stack five or six T-shirts per palette.)

Folding and stacking doesn't work any better in drawers, if that's what you're thinking. The things on the bottom are never worn. You

Above: Proper folding takes the wrinkles out of space planning, making it considerably easier to quickly find what you're looking for. Below: Pull-out palettes made of thin acrylic conserve vertical space when compared to standard shelves. Now there's room for that new sweater.

know what they say about out of sight out of mind. I'll admit it's tempting to stack things in the deep drawers that come standard in most chests or dressers, but it really isn't an efficient use of space. Deep-bottomed drawers are only really good for bulky sweaters or sweats. However, by customizing a lift-out or sliding upper tray you can better utilize the drawer's depth. Store seasonal or infrequently worn items beneath the divider, and use the shallow upper tray to display more-often-used garments such as pajamas, shorts, or swim trunks.

Overall, knit shirts, T-shirts, sweaters, and shorts are better stored on pull-out palettes or in cubbies designed to keep their contents visible and accessible. Watches, tie clips, tuxedo accessories, and the like store well in shallow drawers, particularly if the drawers are fitted with custom or ready-made partitioned inserts.

Other items that work well for drawer storage include socks and underwear. But again, I emphasize the value of proper folding techniques and dividers to get the most economical and functionable use out of drawer storage.

TIES

Oh sure, they look innocent, but organizing ties is the most challenging space-planning problem in a man's closet. The best defense is a good offense. Make it impossible for them to gang up on you. Store ties individually rather than in layers. You should be able to see and reach every tie without disturbing another. Most ready-made tie racks don't accomplish this. Hanging ties in wall closets presents a greater problem, unless you can hang them on the back of the door. And remember there should always be a mirror nearby.

Above: This drop-down tie dowel is available through mail-order catalogs. Right: Eight tie dowels customized into a twelve-inch (30.4cm) -wide pull-out cabinet display over sixty ties in rich retail fashion. A center drawer holds the client's coordinating pocket scarves. The entire unit rests flush against closet cabinetry when not in use.

POSSESSIONS/CLOTHING INVENTORY—HIS

Name: _____ Height: _____ Right-handed: _____ Left-handed: _____

Physical limitations: _____ Highest comfortable reach: Shelf _____

With hanger in hand to: Pole _____

HIS HANGING GARMENTS

CATEGORY	VERTICAL LENGTH (from top of hanger hook to bottom of longest garment)	HORIZONTAL DISTANCES (side to side on pole or number of garments)*	COMMENTS (preferences)
Jumpsuits			
Robes			
Coats			
Outerwear jackets			
Casual jackets			
Sports jackets			
Tuxes			
Suits			
Athletic Outfits			
Slacks/pants			
Jeans/casual			
Dress shirts			
Casual shirts			
Casual shirts/tops			
Polo and T-shirts			
Shorts			
Other			

*See box on page 93

HIS FOLDED GARMENTS

CATEGORY	FOLDED DIMENSIONS OF LARGEST (length x width x height)	HOW MANY (altogether)	COMMENTS (preferences)
T-shirts			
Sweatshirts			
Sweatpants			
Sweaters: Bulky			
Regular			
Shorts			
Swimsuits			
Underpants			
Dress socks			
Athletic socks			
Pajamas			
Scarves			
Gloves			
Handkerchiefs			
Other			

continued on next page

When space planning a man's closet, I use one of these inventory sheets to determine how much horizontal and vertical space each category of clothing and possessions requires. There is also a place to note personal reach and preferences for hanging or folding garments.

POSSESSIONS/CLOTHING INVENTORY—HIS

continued from previous page

HIS ACCESSORIES AND MISCELLANEOUS ITEMS			

CATEGORY	DIMENSIONS OF LARGEST OR LONGEST (length x width x height)	HOW MANY (altogether)	COMMENTS (preferences)
Totebags			
Briefcases			
Belts:			
That hang			
That do not hang			
Ties			
Eyeglasses			
Daily accessories			
Travel accessories:			
Toiletry bags			
Mini appliances			
Other			
Jewelry:			
Rings			
Watches			
Cuff links			
Link bracelets			
Other			
Steamer			
Chair valet			
Hats:			
In hatbox			
Out of hatbox			
Suitcases:			
Large			
Small			
Collapsible			
Shoes:			
Dress			
Casual			
Slippers			
Running/walking/tennis/golf			
Boots and hiking boots			

Many men's accessories and miscellaneous items require special attention when space planning, so it helps to carefully inventory these items as well as to consider life-style or career.

WOMEN'S CLOSETS

You remember Joe Wardrobe? Now meet Joan Wardrobe. Like Joe, she has an average-size closet with average contents. Let's peek inside. She has at least six and as many as twelve different-length garments and what seems to be an infinity of shoes, handbags, scarves, belts, and accessories. Nothing too unusual for a woman's closet. Upon closer examination, we see that her handbags range in size from clutch-size jeweled evening bags to catchall leather totes; the necklines on her shirts and blouses include V-necks, boat necks, portrait, sweetheart, turtleneck, and button-down; her dresses are conservative, strapless, off-the-shoulder, and halter style; Joan's belts measure anywhere from one-quarter inch to six inches

(0.6cm to 15.2cm) wide; her shoe wardrobe might include sandals, flats, low, medium, and high heels, boots of varying heights, and athletic shoes. No wonder women need more than half of the available closet space!

At this juncture, it may be redundant to say that planning a woman's closet requires more resourcefulness than does a man's. After all, there is not much difference between a man's dress and everyday clothes; a tux and a suit are fairly similar with respect to hangers or how much space each requires in the closet. On the other hand, a woman's daytime dresses, cocktail dresses, or evening gowns measure varying lengths and require different types of hangers.

Women's wardrobes come in all lengths. This client, like most women, needed several heights of hanging space. Shoe heels also range in height, so shelves are adjustable. Pull-out acrylic palettes, spaced sparingly, organize hats.

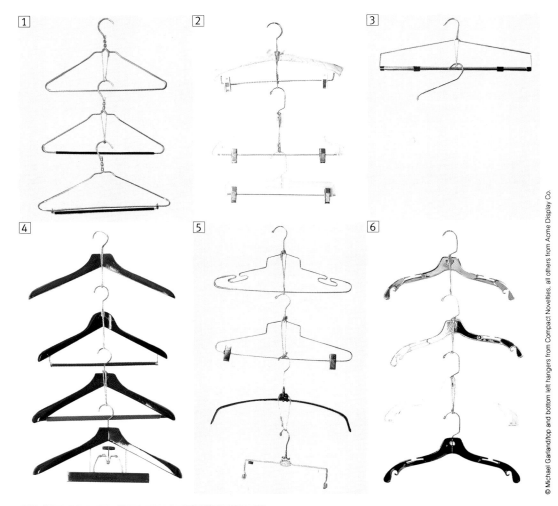

The right hanger is essential. Select the proper one according to the garment and the available space: 1) casual outfits; 2) two-piece outfits, skirts, or slacks; 3) folded tablecloths, pants; 4) men's jackets and suits; 5) skinny hangers for dresses, two-piece outfits, sweaters, or skirts; 6) colorful hangers for dresses, tops, and jackets.

THE TEN COMMANDMENTS (+1) REVISITED

As I said in my opening remarks, there are certain space-planning rules that will improve any closet, construction or no construction. Calculating the right amount of hanging space is particularly important when organizing a woman's closet because she does have so many items of different lengths. Take advantage of space and double-hang short garments whenever possible, reserving single-hanging poles for long gowns, jumpsuits, robes, dresses, and slacks. (Don't forget to put shelves above single-hanging garments!) The first step in space planning is taking inventory. The objective is to determine exactly how much storage you need for each category of clothes and accessories (see the inventory sheets on pages 108 and 109). Finally, a practical use for math!

As you space plan your closet, keep in mind that space is three dimensional; it has height, width, and depth. Don't hang gar-ments—slacks, for example—that measure only sixteen inches (40.6cm) deep in a twenty-six-inch (66cm)-deep space. Okay. Start by inventorying each category of garments, and measuring each horizontally (the width of the entire category) and vertically (the top of the hanger hook to the bottom of the longest garment in each category). To calculate how much double-hanging space you require, group all the short items (forty to forty-two inches [101.6 to 106.6cm] or less) together, add their horizontal measurements, and divide by two. Reserve at least 25 percent more space than you actually need for each category to accommodate new items.

The next step is placement. Group like items (such as blouses) together and put them where they are the most space efficient. Keep items that are worn together—suits and blouses, for example—near each other, especially if you're working around an impediment in your closet.

Buy the right kind of hanger for each garment, taking its dimensions into consideration. Wooden suit or padded gown hangers take up more inches on the pole than do plastic hangers. Similarly, skirt hangers take up less vertical space than do suit hangers. By the way, stay away from multi-unit hangers. They don't make the most efficient use of vertical space, because garments hang so long they cut into double-hanging allotments. It's also inconvenient to access clothes from these hangers without messing up all the others.

Next, count and measure your folded garments so you can plan your shelving needs. In addition to placing shelves above single-hanging items, include a separate section of shelving for larger quantities. Either fold your items to fit the existing space or build custom shelves to accommodate sweaters the way you like to fold them. If your shelf space is narrow and high, fold things so they'll be bulkier. On the other hand, to store folded items on wide not-so-high shelves, fold them so they'll be thinner.

© Michael Garland/Maxine Ordesky, space design

The pièce de résistance of this client's closet is the removable, adjustable pole for extra hangers, which should be kept apart from clothing so as not to waste space or clutter closet hanging poles.

A hallmark of this client's closet was the existing alcove and window. To utilize this unusual space without blocking the window access, I designed a rolling chest of drawers. The large island has a cushioned seat, in-drawer ironing board, and tiny cubbies for miscellaneous storage.

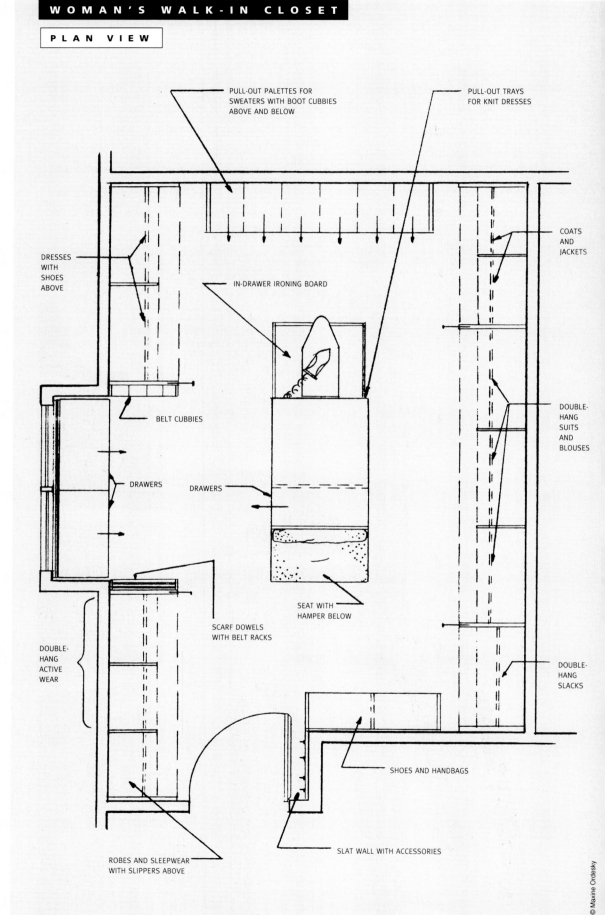

WOMAN'S WALK-IN CLOSET

PLAN VIEW

PULL-OUT PALETTES FOR SWEATERS WITH BOOT CUBBIES ABOVE AND BELOW

PULL-OUT TRAYS FOR KNIT DRESSES

DRESSES WITH SHOES ABOVE

COATS AND JACKETS

IN-DRAWER IRONING BOARD

BELT CUBBIES

DOUBLE-HANG SUITS AND BLOUSES

DRAWERS

DRAWERS

DOUBLE-HANG ACTIVE WEAR

SCARF DOWELS WITH BELT RACKS

SEAT WITH HAMPER BELOW

DOUBLE-HANG SLACKS

SHOES AND HANDBAGS

ROBES AND SLEEPWEAR WITH SLIPPERS ABOVE

SLAT WALL WITH ACCESSORIES

© Maxine Ordesky

HOW MUCH IS ENOUGH?

Predicting the stock market based on women's hemlines may have been fashionable at one time, but doing so today would be a Wall Street faux pas! Hemlines today are as individual and personal as investment strategies, and the numbers below take this into account. I would, however, like to add two disclaimers: (1) our propensity toward shoulder pads has increased the horizontal measurements of many garment categories, and (2) actual measurements will of course vary according to your own figure!

ITEM	LENGTH (from top of hanger hook to bottom of garment)	THICKNESS (each garment including hanger)
Skirts	22"–44" (55.8–111.7cm)	1"–1¹/₂" (2.5–3.8cm)
Suits	22"–42" (55.8–106.6cm)	1¹/₂"–3" (3.8–7.6cm)
Blouses	30"–42" (76.2–106.6cm)	1"–2" (2.5–5cm)
Dresses	48"–66" (121.9–167.6cm)	1"–2" (2.5–5cm)
Jackets	28"–42" (71.1–106.6cm)	1¹/₂"–3" (3.8–7.6cm)
Bathrobes	48"–68" (121.9–172.7cm)	1"–3" (2.5–7.6cm)
Jumpsuits	62"–68" (157.4–172.7cm)	1"–1¹/₂" (2.5–3.8cm)
Slacks	46"–50" (116.8–127cm)	1"–1¹/₂" (2.5–3.8cm)
Shorts	22"–30" (55.8–76.2cm)	1"–1¹/₂" (2.5–3.8cm)
Evening gowns	62"–68" (157.4–172.7cm)	1"–6" (2.5–15.2cm)

HATS

For maximum protection, store hats in sturdy hatboxes. See-through ones are clearly ideal. However, clients with extensive hat collections may prefer display-style storage. I recommend a slat wall with hat fixtures or sometimes even retail display items. Custom cubbies or brim forms also work well for hats.

SCARVES AND SHAWLS

These items are often delicate fabrics requiring special handling. There are three good ways to store scarves or shawls: folded over dowels, hanging from open-end slack hangers, or folded on pull-out palettes. The latter is best if hanging space is at a premium. Of course you can also fold scarves and shawls on shallow shelves; just don't pile them more than two or three high.

BLOUSES AND JACKETS

Boat-neck blouses or those that slip easily should be hung on hangers to which plastic grippers called MK-slips have been added. Padded or curved hangers will also more securely hold blouses and jackets with shoulder pads but be prepared to allot more horizontal inches on the closet pole. Double-hang as much as possible. Organize garments by color and style, keeping business and dress items separate from casual and athletic.

Scarves and other delicate accessories require special handling. Gently fold and store smaller items in partitioned shallow drawers such as these, which I designed for a California client who also needed space for spare eyeglasses.

Above: To keep this client's many long blouses within her reach without wasting vertical storage, I double hung the space, keeping the short items at the bottom. Above right: Eight sweaters in stacks of two fill each of this client's five pull-out trays in a custom-designed island. The island is on wheels for really flexible organizing.

FOLDED SWEATERS

As I discussed before, the trick to storing folded garments is folding them to fit the space. This is equally true for sweaters, T-shirts, and sweats. For access, use pull-out palettes or trays. Lightweight sweaters or those that won't stretch can be hung if your shelf space is limited. Extra-wide pull-out trays are great for three-quarter-length coat sweaters or any sweater that doesn't hang well.

SKIRTS AND SKIRT SUITS

Hang each skirt individually and specifically on a skirt hanger. Your skirts should not hang any longer than they have to. If you have more than one length of skirts, designate a hanging section for each. Above your shortest skirts you can hang your longest blouses and vice versa. Skirt suits take up more length than do single skirts. The most efficient way to hang suits is to use suit hangers and then place them with same-length garments.

SLACKS

There are two ways to properly store slacks: folded over on open-end pant hangers or hanging long on clip hangers or on wooden slat hangers. For delicate fabrics that will crease, long hanging is best. Which way you chose depends upon personal preference and whether or not you have enough vertical space to hang your slacks long. If your closet is short on vertical space, fold your slacks and work them into the double-hanging section of your closet.

DRESSES AND LONG HANGING GARMENTS

It's not unusual for me to designate as many as three or four different single-hanging sections for my client's long garments. In general, if a single category measures at least eighteen inches (45.7cm) wide, a separate hanging section is warranted. By separating same-length garments, you can better plan the overall long hanging space. I put shelves above single-hanging space so clients can store purses, hats, or folded garments near their hanging items.

The number of shelves depends upon how much vertical space the clothes require. Garments measuring fifty-five inches (139.7cm) long on the hanger will yield enough vertical room for three or four shelves starting two inches (5cm) above the pole, whereas those that are only forty-six inches (116.8cm) long would leave enough space to build a fourth or fifth shelf. To maximize vertical hanging space, the bottom of the garments should hang only two to three inches (5 to 7.6cm) above the floor.

BELTS

Believe it or not, women's belts can vary in size from one-quarter inch to six inches (0.6 to 15.2cm) wide. Not all belts hang cooperatively; some must be rolled, others laid flat. I generally design custom cubbies in addition to using racks to hold clients' belts, the idea being that each belt will have its own storage area. If your budget says no to cubbies, try to organize the belts as much as possible—by size, color, and style.

LINGERIE, HOSIERY, AND SOCKS

These garments belong in divided drawers at best or at least in containers on shelves. Again, your objective is to be able to see and reach each item without disturbing another. The organizing purist with well-planned space has drawers in either the closet itself or the bathroom. Packaged hosiery stores easily in closet cubbies.

Courtesy Lillian Vernon

© Michael Garland/Maxine Ordesky, space design

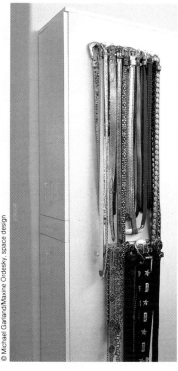

© Michael Garland/Maxine Ordesky, space design

Top: Retail drawer organizers. Above and left: Custom pull-out cubbied units allowed this client to store all her belts together. The center drawer holds rigid belts with big buckles.

© Michael Garland/Maxine Ordesky, space design

Storing shoes toe-in/toe-out (spoon-style) can save enough space to accommodate an extra pair of shoes on each shelf.

SHOES

Do shoes enter your closet, never to be seen again? Women own and wear many types of shoes, which isn't surprising considering the variety of their wardrobes. The first space-planning decision for this category is whether to store them in their original boxes. I say no.

Doing so violates my first commandment: Thou shalt see everything. But if you persist in storing your shoes this way, make one of two possible improvements. Either invest in see-through shoe containers or slit the labeled end of the cardboard box so you can simply slide the shoes in or out without tumbling the entire stack.

By the way, if you're storing shoes in boxes to keep them dust-free, maybe you aren't wearing them often enough to justify keeping them. Do they still fit you? Are they fashionable? The only infrequently worn shoes that you should store are those that match only one or two specific outfit(s) or are very dressy.

Sans shoe boxes, you have several storage options. The most space-efficient method is the heel-to-heel technique. It works best, however, on shelves that are within your comfortable reach. Positioning one shoe of each pair behind its mate is a good storage strategy for the shelf immediately above single-hanging closet poles. Obviously, this technique works only on shelves where you can reach the back. Remember the shelf must be at least twenty inches (50.8cm) deep.

Depending upon your shelf length and shoe width, you can save as much as one to one and a half inches (2.5 to 3.8cm) per pair by using the toe-in/toe-out method. Multiplying that savings by several pairs on the same shelf creates enough room to store another pair. Position your shoe shelves at the proper height for the shoes, eliminating as much air space as possible between shelves. Of course, over-the-door shoe racks or pocketed bags make the most space sense in small wall closets with standard doors. I don't recommend shoe holders designed to rest on the closet floor, unless of course you have no other choice. If this is your situation, then shoe racks are preferable to merely putting the shoes loose on the floor.

BATHROBES AND SLIPPERS

Nightgowns and pajamas can be hung or folded. If you prefer the former, be sure you

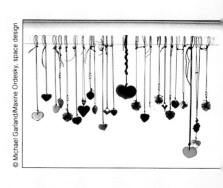

have the right hangers so the garments don't slip off. Dress and blouse hangers with notched shoulders are good for nightgowns but pj's need suit hangers with clips or a bar on which to hang folded pants. I prefer to set aside a separate single-hanging section for sleepwear, with shelves above for slippers. This particular section should, for most lifestyles, be up front and available in a closet. Barring that, at least install some hooks near the door for that oft-used comfortable robe.

HANDBAGS

Like everything else in a woman's closet, handbags come in all sizes and shapes, so it is best to organize them according to category and size. Cubbies with removable partitions are the best way to store purses and totes because you can reconfigure them as your collection changes. Store bags upright on their sturdiest side. Soft-bottom purses can be upended to rest on their framed top. Small bags might even fit in drawers. With shoulder bags, always put the straps inside so they don't tangle on other bags when you take them in and out of their storage area. Some women like to keep their stored bags stuffed with tissue. If space is a luxury, there's no reason not to.

I certainly understand the need to protect bags from scuffing, but remember, leather needs to breathe. No Baggies! You can prevent scuffing by lining cubbies or shelves with felt or similar fabric. But handbags in cloth bags is akin to shoes in their boxes: no visibility. If dust is more of a problem than scuffing, then refer to my foolproof remedy for dusty shoes!

JEWELRY AND HAIR ACCESSORIES

When organizing and storing these items, make sure you have fun! Jewelry and hair accessories are so lovely, why not enjoy them? Unless security is an issue, consider custom-making or buying wall-hung acrylic jewelry containers, replete with hooks for necklaces and shelves for smaller items. Of course, felt-, velvet-, or synthetic-suede-lined drawer inserts (retail or custom) also work well for jewelry. If you have counter or shelf space, you might want to buy retail display items to keep your jewelry visible and handy (see sources at the back of the book).

Hair accessories such as decorative combs, clips, barrettes, and headbands are awkward to store in a uniform manner because they are such different shapes and sizes. On small shelves or cubbies they become works of art. In drawers, they will need partitions to maintain order. Headbands can be stored attractively on hooks or even dowels. Both jewelry and hair accessories can be placed in the closet or bathroom, wherever space allows and as personal habits dictate. Just be sure there's a mirror nearby!

Above: This client's collection of heart necklaces dangles from a custom-measured acrylic pole designed to organize and display her pieces. It's supported by wires and hung in front of an opaque window. Above left: Cubbies can hold packaged hoisery as well as handbags upright. Left: A retail acrylic jewelry organizer has functional slide-out panels.

POSSESSIONS/CLOTHING INVENTORY—HERS

Name: _____ Height: _____ Right-handed: _____ Left-handed: _____

Physical limitations: _____ Highest comfortable reach: Shelf _____

With hanger in hand to: Pole _____

HER HANGING GARMENTS

CATEGORY	VERTICAL LENGTH (from top of hanger hook to bottom of longest garment)	HORIZONTAL DISTANCES (side to side on pole or number of garments)*	COMMENTS (preferences)
Jumpsuits			
Robes			
Nightgowns			
Coats			
Outerwear jackets			
Casual jackets (not part of suit)			
Daytime dresses			
Dressy dresses			
Suits (one on a hanger)			
or Separate jackets			
Separate skirts			
Dressy skirt outfits (one on a hanger)			
or Separate tops			
Separate skirts			
Casual skirt outfits (one on a hanger)			
or Separate tops			
Separate skirts			
Dressy pants outfits (one on a hanger)			
or Separate tops			
Separate pants			
Casual pants outfits (one on a hanger)			
or Separate tops			
Separate pants			
Shirts: Short			
Long			
Slacks			
Jogging/athletic (one on a hanger)			
or Separate tops			
Separate pants			
Dressy tops/blouses			
Tennis outfits			
Shorts			
Other			

*See box on page 103

HER FOLDED GARMENTS

CATEGORY	FOLDED DIMENSIONS OF LARGEST (length x width x height)	HOW MANY (altogether)	COMMENTS (preferences)
T-shirts			
Sweatshirts			
Sweatpants			
Sweaters: Bulky			
Regular			
Shawls			
Folded knit dress			

This is a sample of the inventory sheet I use for my women clients. Taking inventory is just as important to good space planning as learning about a client's life-style and obtaining his or her wish list for dream closets.

continued on next page

her folded garments continued

CATEGORY	FOLDED DIMENSIONS OF LARGEST (length x width x height)	HOW MANY (altogether)	COMMENTS (preferences)
Sweatpants			
Shorts			
Leotards & body suits			
Swimsuits			
Bras			
Teddys			
Underpants			
Slips			
Pajamas			
Nightgowns			
Panty hose			
Packaged hose			
Knee-high hose			
Regular socks			
Athletic socks			
Scarves			
Gloves			
Handkerchiefs			
Other			

HER ACCESSORIES AND MISCELLANEOUS ITEMS

CATEGORY	DIMENSIONS OF LARGEST (length x width x height)	HOW MANY (altogether)	COMMENTS (preferences)
Handbags: Evening			
Regular			
Tote type			
Belts: That hang			
That do not hang			
Hair ornaments			
Eyeglasses and cases			
Handbag accessories			
Travel accessories: Toiletry bags			
Mini appliances			
Other			
Jewelry: Rings			
Watches			
Earrings			
Link bracelets			
Necklaces			
Other			
Steamer			
Chair valet			
Hats: In hatbox			
Out of hatbox			
Suitcases: Large			
Small			
Collapsible			
Shoes: High heels			
Flats			
Slippers			
Running/walking/tennis/golf			
Boots and hiking boots			

Women's numerous accessories and miscellaneous items are varied to suit the many life-styles and career opportunities today's woman enjoys. When consulting with a client and inventorying her possessions, I try to include as many of these items as possible.

© Maxine Ordesky

CHILDREN'S CLOSETS

The space-planning principles used to organize adults' closets apply to children's closets as well, only on a smaller scale: maximize vertical and horizontal space, make it adjustable, and use the right hangers. In kid's closets, however, I encourage floor-level storage for large toys.

Essentially, the same space planning and organizing rules that govern adults' closets apply to children's closets: Make it adjustable; store things within easy reach; use correctly sized hangers; and on average, girls' closets will be more complex than boys' closets. The only rule for adults' closets that doesn't make sense for children's is keeping things off the floor. The floor in a child's closet is anything but taboo. It's the ideal place to put pull-and-push toys or rolling storage bins. Remember, the most important element in organizing a child's closet is putting things where they can reach them.

Like everything in a growing child's world, closets can also be a learning environment. When you or your space planner designs your child's closet, keep in mind that the easier it is for your child to use, the quicker he or she will learn to stay organized and take responsibility for his or her belongings. For example, it's much easier for children to keep clothing neat and wrinkle free if they don't have stacks of items eight to ten inches (20.3 to 25.4cm) high or adult hangers crammed onto an overcrowded closet pole that they can't reach. Provide places for your child to put dirty clothes (even

CHILD'S CLOSET

ELEVATION

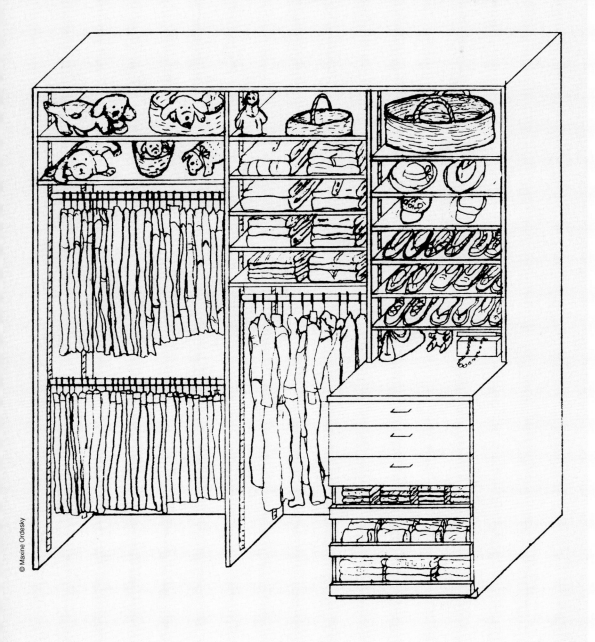

© Maxine Ordesky

CAPACITY

Skirts and pants	4'-0" (1.2m)	Folded garments	30	
Tops and jackets	4'-0" (1.2m)	Drawers	12	
Dresses and coats	2'-0" (0.6m)	Palettes	36	
		Shoes	46 pairs	
Total hanging	10'-0" (3m)	Stuffed animals	Lots	

Even at a young age, it's evident how varied women's wardrobes are. This client's preteen daughter already required three different heights of hanging space. Frequently worn items are kept in open pull-out trays where they can be seen and easily reached when she's in a hurry.

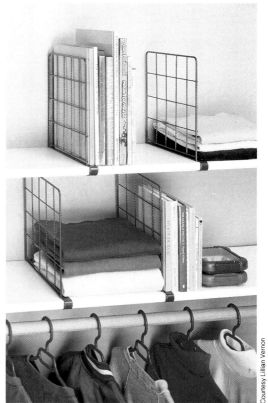

if it's only a plastic basket on the floor), to hang what should be hung, and to fold what can be folded. Making the closet adjustable allows you to reconfigure the space with extra shelves and poles as your child's wardrobe and toys change. Still not sold on the virtues of adjustability?

Just reflect for a moment on how adjustable children are, how quickly they grow, and how from the time they're newborns, they'll have clothes of many different sizes. People love to give baby clothes for the months and years ahead. Infants' and toddlers' clothes are short enough to be triple-hung. But soon after that, you'll need considerably longer hanging space—I was very surprised by how quickly my two boys outgrew "foldable" trouser sizes. Again, an adjustable system of shelves and poles made it much easier to maintain a space-efficient closet.

The photographs on these pages illustrate several specific ways to organize and maximize storage in a child's closet. Take advantage of horizontal, eye-level spaces. Use higher shelves to store things your child doesn't need to reach and small areas such as side

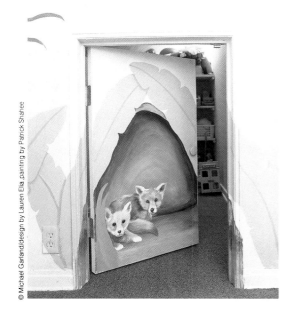

© Michael Garland/design by Lauren Elia, painting by Patrick Shahee

returns for short shelves to hold tiny shoes or toys.

One final note: My maternal instincts nudge me to address safety. Children of all ages will explore, play, and roughhouse from time to time. Small children in particular love to climb. Consequently, be sure adjustable shelves are safe. There is a locking shelf support available to keep these adjustable shelves from tipping should your child turn them into a makeshift ladder. Although hooks placed at eye level on the inside of closet doors are ideal hanging spaces for a child's jacket or robe, avoid long sharp hooks that could be dangerous.

© Lois Ellen Frank/Maxine Ordesky, space design

Opposite left: Shoes, clothes, games, and toys share a well-planned, flexible wall closet in a boy's bedroom. Shirts are folded in short stacks for easy access and minimal maintenance. Opposite right: Retail partitions fit over shelves for a quick space-planning retrofit. This page, above left: This child's toy closet is a private den. Left: This photograph of the illustration on page 111 shows space planning in action. A preteen's shoe collection can expand into open pull-out trays with socks filling empty drawers above.

CHAPTER SIX

LAUNDRY AND UTILITY ROOMS

Left: Dividing this client's wall closet into two spaces was the first step toward a utility closet that houses adjustable shelves, a rolling step stool, wall-mounted brooms, mops, and vacuum attachments, and an on-door caddy for the ironing board.

Despite what some young children—and oblivious teenagers—seem to believe, clean clothes don't magically materialize in dresser drawers. In reality, something happens between the time dirty clothes are removed and returned to the closet all fresh and clean. And that "thing" happens in the laundry room. This area of your home may be a mystery to some family members, but if you're the primary user, you could probably do a load of wash in your sleep. Come to think of it, that would be a pretty neat trick!

Laundry rooms rarely receive the attention they deserve (kind of like the people who so diligently use them on behalf of others). Laundry rooms aren't living spaces or private sanctuaries or places where meals are prepared or bodies bathed. No wonder most families find better ways to spend their home-improvement dollars. Still, laundry rooms—utility rooms or mudrooms as they're sometimes called—warrant space planning, if for no other reason than to lighten the load. But there are other reasons, too. Here are a few.

1 Potentially harmful chemicals are stored and used there.

2 They're small spaces cramped by large appliances that might require repair or removal.

3 They're rooms that end up as cluttered, catchall areas.

4 They're susceptible to ventilation and plumbing problems.

5 Cleaning supplies aren't all the same size and need different storage space.

6 Powdered or liquid soap can make a mess if spilled.

7 Cleaning and laundry supplies bought in bulk are awkward to move so they should be stored conveniently and in a usable manner.

8 If your laundry room is really together, it'll be much easier to teach other family members to do their own wash!

PLANNING A LAUNDRY ROOM

Does your laundry room depress you? Doing laundry is probably not a top-ten activity; it's a chore, right? But if your laundry room is well planned and organized, it can give you a sense of accomplishment and take the sting out of doing the wash. By now you already know the

PLANNING A LAUNDRY ROOM

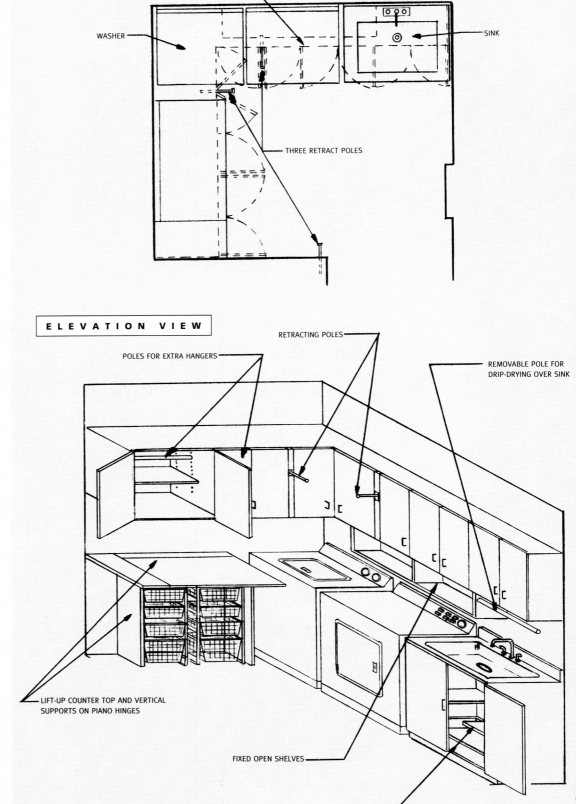

PLAN VIEW

DRYER

WASHER

SINK

THREE RETRACT POLES

ELEVATION VIEW

RETRACTING POLES

POLES FOR EXTRA HANGERS

REMOVABLE POLE FOR DRIP-DRYING OVER SINK

LIFT-UP COUNTER TOP AND VERTICAL SUPPORTS ON PIANO HINGES

FIXED OPEN SHELVES

SIDE SHELVES AND PULL-OUT TRAY

© Maxine Ordesky

These drawings demonstrate how much space planning can go into the often-ignored laundry room, which is typically small and full of large appliances. The benefits in terms of organization and efficiency are overwhelming.

first step to space planning and organizing: identification. Think about everything you have to do and would like to do in your dream laundry room. Be realistic about whether or not the room is large enough to accommodate all the activities you'd like to do there, such as clothes sorting, ironing, sewing, gift wrapping, feeding family pets, and so on.

Also include these issues.

1 Where are dirty clothes put in your home and how do they get to the laundry room?

2 Do you want separate hampers for pre-sorting?

3 Do you wash a number of clothes that require special handling?

4 Do you want counter space for folding clothes?

5 Who irons the clothes in your family, and what sort of ironing facilities are necessary?

6 Are your machines top- or front-loading?

7 How often do you do laundry and ironing?

8 Do you purchase large quantities of laundry supplies?

Because laundry rooms are usually adjacent to a back or side door, they unwittingly become the stopping point for all incoming and outgoing foot traffic. Having grown up in Massachusetts, I can tell you that on cold winter days nary a hot chocolate was sipped until we removed our messy boots and coats in the mudroom, alias the laundry room. We also deposited our mittens, schoolbooks, and a host of other childhood treasures there. No wonder it was always so messy, despite my mother's efforts to keep it organized.

Well, now that I'm a professional space planner and organizer, I realize the errors of our ways. Fortunately, today's laundry

This client's laundry room (plan opposite) defines space planning. A removable sink cover serves as a table, detergent and supplies are stored near appliances, a hanging pole between cabinets retracts, and corner cabinets open out from center.

© Lois Ellen Frank/Maxine Ordesky, space design

In an organized laundry room, a wall-mounted phone frees up counter space, a work surface flips up for washer repairs, spare hangers dangle from a removable pole in an upper cabinet, and the hamper glides for convenience.

rooms and/or mudrooms enjoy the benefits of improved design and space-saving products.

WHERE DO YOU DO LAUNDRY?

In an ideal, organized, and space-planned world, a laundry room is exactly that—a room with ample space for doing laundry and everything related to it. There's room for your washer, dryer, soaps, and softeners, a sink for hand washing, a pole for drip drying, an ironing board, extra hangers, and maybe even a sewing kit. What I classify as the crème de la crème of laundry rooms is one that is fully equipped and located adjacent to the kitchen or in the basement. In newer two-story homes, the laundry room is sometimes on the

second floor, nearer to the bedrooms. In warm climates, laundry rooms can be au naturel. It's common to find washers and dryers in the garage or even beneath a carport.

In apartments or homes with very limited space, laundry rooms are often reduced to closets; tiny spaces with just room enough for a side-by-side washer and dryer. In extreme space crunches, laundry closets can shrink to laundry corners where there's barely space enough for a stacking washer/dryer unit. I've visited homes where the washer and dryer are pushed into a kitchen pantry, an alcove, or beneath a countertop and hidden behind cabinet doors. Future remodelers could think about closing in a porch or extending a hallway just enough to accommodate a small but well-equipped laundry room.

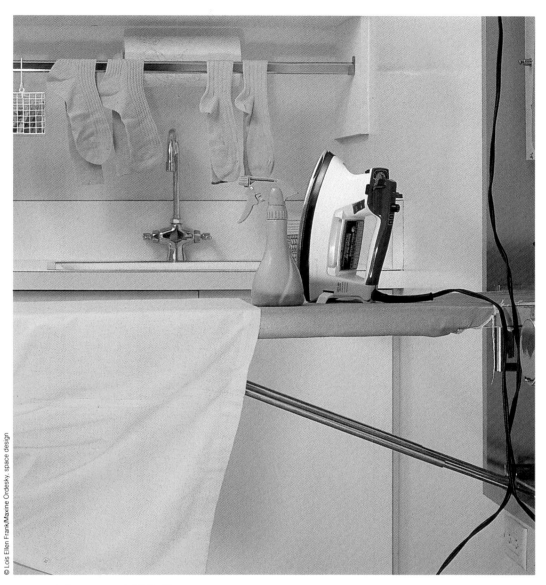

© Lois Ellen Frank/Maxine Ordesky, space design

A PICTURE-PERFECT LAUNDRY ROOM

At the very least, a laundry room needs a washer and dryer. That's obvious. At the most, it should have everything you need to make doing laundry less of a chore—assuming that's possible! Here are some of the features found in my ideal laundry room.

Overhead cabinets are a must in any laundry room or laundry closet. A full-size washer and dryer measure approximately five feet (1.5m) when positioned side by side. Installing cabinets above them yields five feet (1.5m) of storage space times the number of shelves! Three shelves roughly equals fifteen feet (4.5m) of beautiful and new storage space.

Corner cabinets designed to utilize that trouble spot feature doors that open toward one another to display their entire contents at one time.

A hinged countertop swings down into action as an extra work surface and flips up out of the way to allow access to the washer for repair. This is a great technique because it creates an instant folding table without creating an obstacle to the washer.

Full-size appliances fit comfortably side by side in a well-planned laundry room. Additionally, they are conveniently accessible for repairs or removal if necessary.

An ironing center complete with an iron and an extra light pops down from the wall when needed and stores effortlessly away when not in use. In small spaces, you can also install fold-down ironing boards that

HAS ANYONE SEEN THE VACUUM? AND OTHER UTILITY CLOSET NIGHTMARES

When things go bump in the night, check your utility closet in the morning—assuming of course you can open the door without everything toppling out. Face it, utility closets aren't always the best-organized spot in the house. But they could be. Sooner or later, you should actually need everything you stow there, especially that screw you found six months ago. Only things you use belong in the utility closet. So throw away the stray screw....

Seriously, utility closets are a luxury. If the closet god bestowed upon your home an entire closet that doesn't have to hold anything but a few mops, brooms, and general household and cleaning supplies, make the most of it! Install adjustable and/or pull-out shelves so you can maximize storage space. Remember to make room for tall items too.

People aren't careful about how they put things away in closets. But you can combat this enemy by making it perfectly obvious where everything belongs. Cleaning supplies here, pet food in that caddy, extra vacuum bags on the wall next to the upright. Again, with all the available mail-order and retail closet-organizing products, it's easy to utilize your utility closet.

This self-contained ironing center, which is available commercially, stores flush against the wall, and the leg-free design is easier for pressing larger items. Finally, I included a rod above the sink for drip-drying delicates or air-drying stubborn socks.

hang on the back of doors or models that unfold from pull-out drawers or collapse small enough to slide between your machines or under a countertop.

A short removable rod for drip drying hangs above the sink, which can be covered with a custom-made top in order to double as a flat work surface.

Retracting poles in narrow stiles between cabinet sections provide space to hang ironed garments or larger drip-dry items.

An open under-cabinet shelf holds deter-

gents and cleaning-supply caddies neat and within reach.

Extra hangers are hung on a pole in an extra-deep cabinet. Regular hangers measure sixteen inches (40.6cm) from side to side; so a pole installed in a cabinet with an overall depth of eighteen inches (45.7cm) (give or take a little) is plenty of room to store extra hangers.

A rolling hamper makes loading the washer easy. Mail-order catalogs offer several styles, including ones that are divided horizontally or vertically.

Never refuse help with the laundry...especially help from store-bought items such as these. Clockwise, from top left: A hanging caddy for organizing iron-ing board, iron, and starch clears floor space. A rolling drying rack collapses for easy storage yet holds a large quantity of laundry. A cabinet or bathroom pull-man can be retrofitted with well-ventilated sliding bas-ket. A compartmentalized hamper encourages every-one to sort dirty clothes by color.

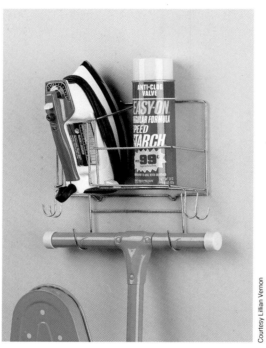

Courtesy Lillian Vernon

Courtesy Lillian Vernon

© Lois Ellen Frank/hamper by Heller

© Courtesy Crystal Cabinet Works Inc.

Courtesy Ikea

ACCESSORIZING AND ORGANIZING THE MUDROOM

You say you like the idea of a mudroom but somehow your kids haven't quite grasped the concept? Tired of wet, muddy boots leaving their marks on the dryer? In the immortal words of a great consumer advocate, "Fight back!" That's right. Trick your mudroom trekkers into keeping the place clean and do it stylishly. The products shown on this page are only a few of the things you can buy for brightening and organizing a mudroom.

Utilize all the space you have. Build a bench with a lift-up seat and storage below. Kids have somewhere to sit; you have somewhere to store cleaning supplies. A small closet near your garage or a back door could be assigned to mudroom patrol simply by removing the closet door and sprucing it up with some of the items shown here. Of course, you'll want to be sure there's plenty of lighting. Mudrooms make great staging areas for everyone. Again because mud-

rooms see a lot of pass-through traffic and are generally near the garage, leave space to temporarily hold dry cleaning, groceries, and other items on their way in or out of the house.

Courtesy Ikea

Courtesy Plow & Hearth

Any one of these retail storage and organizing items will perform spotlessly in the mudroom as well as near front- or backdoor entrances, in breezeways, garages, or laundry rooms. They're all useful for keeping coats or boots organized and accessible.

HOME OFFICES

Left: A freestanding desk in a home library works well as an occasional office. Above: For a client who is an interior designer, I put a forty-four-inch (111.7cm)-deep closet to work. A little space planning, a few adjustable shelves, and a custom desk did the job.

It is the best of rooms; it is the worst of rooms. With all due respect to Dickens, this is a reasonable, if not dramatic, declaration about home offices. Their strong points—proximity to home, fewer time and schedule constraints, a casual work environment—are ironically the home office's weak points as well. When the office is as close as the end of the hall or a flight of stairs, it's hard to shift gears. You're always tempted to pop in and extinguish one more fire, even on weekends. While working in a casual home office is comfortable and enables you to control your distractions, some people find it difficult to motivate themselves in an informal atmosphere.

Pluses and minuses notwithstanding, working at home is on the rise. Today, a fully equipped home office and the preference to work there is often a selling point to a prospective employer. Computer and office-equip-ment companies cater to the domestic entrepreneur, developing products and services specifically for this burgeoning market.

My office and home were one and the same for years, albeit in a makeshift manner that included the dining room table until my youngest son moved into his own apartment. Like most work-at-home professionals, I endured a love-hate relationship with my office. I appreciated the quiet and convenience but far too frequently whole weeks passed before I left the house, let alone my office! Fortunately, my work took me to job sites fairly regularly and clients came to my office so I didn't suffer the same professional isolation that afflicts many homebound nine-to-fivers.

Space planning my home office was the turning point in the love-hate relationship. When I abandoned the dining room table for my son's room, I thought I'd never grow into all that space. Soon enough, though, I was lusting for more file cabinets and bigger work surfaces. Coincidentally, clients who had hired me to space plan their closets and kitchens

POSSIBLE HOME OFFICE LOCATIONS

SECTION

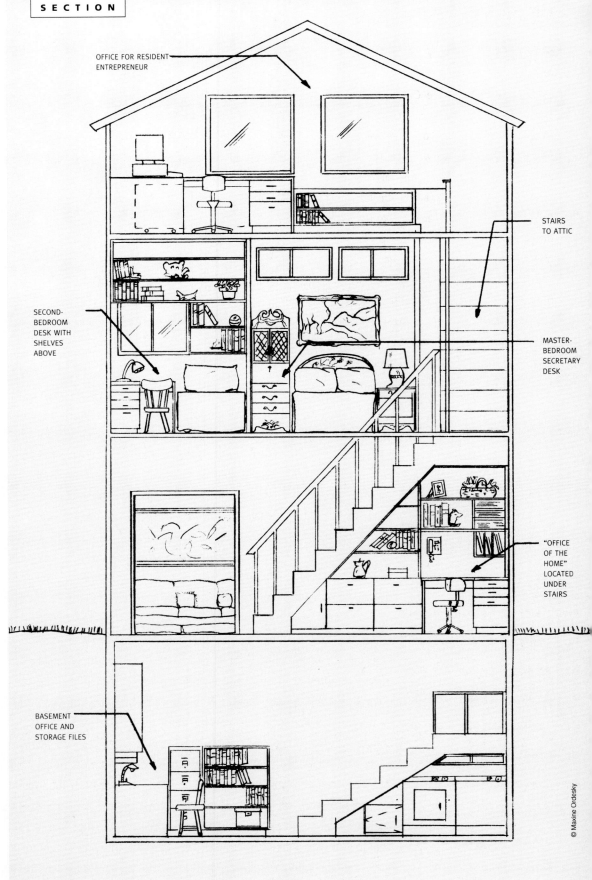

OFFICE FOR RESIDENT ENTREPRENEUR

STAIRS TO ATTIC

SECOND-BEDROOM DESK WITH SHELVES ABOVE

MASTER-BEDROOM SECRETARY DESK

"OFFICE OF THE HOME" LOCATED UNDER STAIRS

BASEMENT OFFICE AND STORAGE FILES

Be imaginative when searching for home office space, even if you need only a bedside table. Look up, down, into closets, and under stairs. Consider how much—or how little—space you really need.

© Maxine Ordesky

called me back to design their home offices. Practicing what I was preaching made it a lot easier for me to keep preaching!

BREAKING GROUND ON A HOME OFFICE

To begin with, here are Ordesky's doctrines of the home office. (1) They are complex, unique rooms. (2) Organization does not occur by osmosis. (3) How-to-work-at-home kits and executive newsletters that extol the virtues of "telecommuting" won't automatically make your home office productive. Only you can accomplish that with the help of proper space planning and good organization from the beginning.

When you set up shop at home, you'll find that it's a tad easier to hang up your shingle than it is in an out-of-the-house office. You already know the neighborhood and the garage provides rent-free storage. However, the manner in which you'll use the space is just as important whether you work at home or rent space elsewhere. Keep in mind that there are two basic kinds of offices. Start by asking yourself which type you need.

HOME OFFICE A

This is a "full-time" office dedicated primarily, if not exclusively, to conducting the business of your profession. These home offices are generally self-contained within one room and separate from the rest of the house. They may even be detached from the home in a guest house, a bungalow, a garage, a garden shed, or a custom-built structure. Type-A home offices typically require more files and overall space than do type-B offices, which I describe next.

© Michael Garland/Maxine Ordesky, space design (all photos)

Left and three views below: For this busy Hollywood executive, I devoted part of a small guest room to office space. The U-shaped configuration and custom-designed shelves with pull-out stationery palettes enhance efficiency. A hinged panel hides wires.

This page: You can never have too many drawers, as these New York clients can attest. My design for their shared bedroom desk has two banks of desk drawers, a kneehole drawer, extra filing drawers on the side, and bureau drawers to hold folded garments on the back.

HOME OFFICE B

This is a "part-time" office in that the space is not used exclusively for business and sometimes it's not used for business at all. These offices might be command central for home-related paperwork, sewing, even late-night study sessions, for example. Type-B offices are generally small, simple, and tucked wherever there's room. You may find one in a kitchen nook, beneath a stairway, or at the far end of the family room concealed by a tall bookcase.

The distinctions between A and B aren't hard and fast. However, each type of at-home work area requires space planning and fore-thought depending upon its primary use. Everyone holds a personal vision of the ideal home office; the essential features of my space differ drastically from those of a pho-tographer's. Once you've decided what type of home office you need, you'll know how much room you require and what equipment you'll be utilizing. Ask yourself certain ques-tions about potential home office locations.

1. Is it a room where the existing furniture can remain in place or can it be removed according to your needs?

2. Will access to your desk and chair be easy? Is there a usable closet in the room?

3. Is there enough wall space for storage units and/or shelving?

4. Is there adequate lighting and good ventilation?

5. Is there room for employees if you need to hire anyone?

6. What office equipment will you need?

7. Are there sufficient and conveniently located outlets? Does your office equipment require a dedicated outlet?

8. Will you install a business phone (with an answering machine and fax) that's separate from your residential lines?

9. Do you want to answer the residence line in your office and vice versa?

ORGANIZING YOUR HOME OFFICE

Space-planning a home office is important. Usually you're dealing with less space than you want and need. When space-planning a home office of any size, first identify the biggest problem that needs resolution. Although space-planning problems could be specific to your work habits or profession, the following seem to be the most common.

1. The size and compatibility of equipment and relevant furniture.

2. Filing space (portable, permanent, temporary) and shelves.

3. Paper flow and traffic patterns.

4. Accommodations for working with clients or employees.

5. Any structural impediments or limitations within the chosen space.

Consider your idiosyncrasies. One advantage of working at home is that you can truly customize the space. Will you want to look out a window? Are you uncomfortable working with your back to the door? Are you right- or left-handed? What daily or less frequent distractions do you anticipate? Where will you place the telephone on the desk? Home offices are more flexible than kitchens or bathrooms because there are no plumbing or gas lines to relocate, so treat yourself to personal pleasantries, whatever they may be.

I designed one client's home office in her oversize bathroom, because she made all her business calls while dressing! Now she's more organized than ever; everything she needs to make her calls is within her reach every morn-

Courtesy Ikea

Courtesy Williams-Sonoma

WHAT IS A DESK?

A desk by any other name is still a desk. Or is it? In a home office, a desk can be a countertop, a door placed horizontally on filing cabinets, an antique table or a brand-new one. Regardless, your home office desk should be storage-intensive so that you can keep all your relevant possessions within it. Why waste all that wonderful, usable empty undercounter space? If your desk is only a table, buy rolling file carts or pedestals to put beneath it.

I believe you get the most workable office space from a desk and return configured in an L- or U-shape. Credenzas fit well into these configurations or by themselves along a wall behind the desk. Custom credenzas are ideal because they can be designed to function in tandem with the desk. However, keep in mind the point I make on page 129 about the wisdom in placing furniture around the office's perimeter, especially if two or more people work simultaneously in the home office.

If you don't have space for a full-size desk, think creatively. A simple table placed at a right angle to the bookshelf may serve the purpose. In an odd-shaped room, an odd-shaped desk, such as the triangular table, makes most sense.

It's always nice to furnish your home office with a table and chairs separate from the desk for use as a conference area or extra work surface when your desk gets temporarily cluttered. Similarly, a large home office might also benefit from a sitting area or sofa.

Far left and left: Home offices often have to share space in rooms that also serve some other purpose. Therefore, freestanding adjustable storage and work units are one option for organizing career and personal needs.

HOME OFFICE BASICS

At the very least, a home office—
Type A or B—requires the following.

- A desk or work surface
- A comfortable chair
- A phone and answering machine
- Filing space
- Writing implements (pens, pencils, computers, and typewriters)
- Supplies (tape, paper clips, stapler and staples, scissors, and so on)
- Drawers
- Shelves
- A wastebasket
- Lighting
- Electric outlets
- A clock
- A calculator

Architect: Christopher H. Rudolph, AIA Chicago, II/Photo: Jessie Walker (both photos)

Above right: Arranging desk and shelves against a wall leaves space for other pieces, as pictured in this guest room/office. Right: Clever space planning tucks linen storage out of sight in under-bed drawers and headboard panel. Opposite: Gather ye office space where ye can. Custom furnish odd-shaped areas. Here, an angled desk aligns with the wall cabinet, creating workspace and a sizable passageway.

ing. The idea is to make your home office productive, whether you run a multimillion-dollar business, local charity events, or your household.

In a well-planned home office, ideally in any office, the tricks of your trade should be at arm's length. Once seated at your desk, you shouldn't have to stand up for any supplies or equipment. Your phone, phone numbers, paper, writing instruments, computer, typewriter, wastebasket, files, and any other paraphernalia of your profession should be no farther away than a comfortable stretch or an effortless swivel.

Two factors will make this possible or impossible, as the case may be: storage and configuration. The type and amount of storage in your office affects productivity. The goal is to have as much storage as possible without detracting from the look and feel of your office. Storage needs and available space impact the furniture and cabinets you buy or build, which in turn influence room configuration. Of course, tasks, work habits,

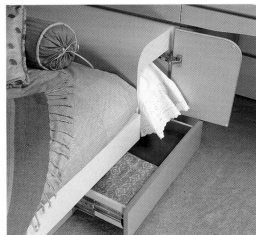

and the number of personnel also affect furniture and cabinet positioning. Let's first look at the many ways of introducing storage into the home office.

OFFICE STORAGE AT HOME

It's been my experience that home office storage and configuration evolve—an old dresser put here, an end table put there. One reason for this may be that people like you and me have trouble gaining access to high-end office furniture such as those lines designed by commercial furniture manufacturers. Of course architects and interior designers can buy what's known as contract office furniture. The extra cost may be worth it; most contract office furniture is exceptionally well designed and appointed.

Barring this route, your choices for professional-looking home office furniture include modular, custom, custom manufactured, and the various species of desks, chairs, and pedestals found at office supply stores. I prefer a gentle mix of residential and office furniture. I used an old highboy in my office to hold stationery, brochures, office supplies, flat artwork, and other appropriately sized items. I enjoyed the homey ambiance it added to the room. Besides being too awkward to move and having no place else to put it, the chest was storage just waiting to happen.

If you have tables that are high enough to slide drawer storage pedestals under, use them in your home office. Who says you have to invest in all-new furniture? Of course, if you want your home office to have a professional feel, you should buy professional office

furniture. Personally, I like the eclectic look of residential and office pieces.

Regardless of how you furnish your home office, I think it's best to arrange as many pieces as possible around the room's perimeter. Office equipment included. This configuration generally yields a more open feeling, which I personally prefer. It's also a nice arrangement if two or more people work simultaneously in the space. Perimeter positioning, as opposed to configurations that jut into the center of the room, make it easier for everyone to work in the space and to walk around one another.

For effective time management and accurate billing, I consider clocks, several clocks, a must-have home office item. I find it expedient to see the time from anywhere in my office, regardless of which work area I'm occupying. Of course you also need whatever specialized items your profession demands. The list is endless and everything needs a home. It's best if you store these easily lost, clutter-making items in partitioned drawers or in specially designed desk accessories.

HOME OFFICE STORAGE IDEAS

Here are several, but certainly not all of the ways to maximize home office storage space. Some involve more carpentry than others, but keep in mind that custom-built office furniture is the best way to maximize storage and floor space.

[1] Above the desk within a section of a shelving unit, install one-quarter-inch (0.6cm) acrylic pull-out palettes to store stationery, periodicals, files, scripts, legal briefs, newsletters, and so on. Palettes need to be only two or three inches (5 to 7.6cm) apart. Placing stationery and other items on palettes frees a desk drawer or shelf for other use and holds papers neat and visible.

[2] Devote at least one twelve-inch (30.4cm)-deep desk drawer to hold hanging files. Complete the "pedestal" or drawer bank with space-efficient shallow drawers. Drawers can be flush-bottom, which will save space.

[3] Use your walls as makeshift bookshelves. If your desk or another table rests up against the wall, you can lean books and reference material against the wall.

[4] Buy rolling file cabinets or carts for current file storage. Select models with enclosed sides so your papers won't fall out when you move the unit.

[5] Use retail drawer organizers to keep contents neat and accessible. Removable partitions are always good because they allow you to reorganize the contents as needs change.

[6] Build shallow shelves onto or into wall returns to hold smaller supplies. Buy or build shelves to fit into corners or under windows or onto walls above desktops.

[7] Custom-build your desk to maximize storage and work space. The deluxe desk shown on page 126 boasts seven more drawers than a ready-made desk of identical proportions. Of course, shallow bookshelves could replace the four back drawers if you require open storage space.

[8] Build a worktable or work station to fit the exact dimensions of a space that is awkward or smaller than standard and gain extra work surface plus the storage space beneath.

[9] Buy or build cabinets or bookshelves to fit under or between windows.

[10] Gain writing or conference space by adding an extension, leaf, or pull-out to the end or side of your desk.

Design: Ruschman Elliot Interior Design, Winnetka, Il/Photo: Mikos of Jessie Walker & Associates

CHAPTER EIGHT

HALLWAYS AND LANDINGS

Implicit in space planning your home is indeed planning to use all the available storage space. Hallways and landings are often overlooked as potential storage windfalls. Bookcases or display shelves are natural storage solutions because they can be built or purchased to fit a specific space. Desks with shelves above or benches with underseat storage fit quite nicely into certain landing and hallway configurations. If you're "under construction," consider invading the interior wall space between the wall studs to build hallway storage. The following pictures ought to inspire you to use hallways and landings to their fullest.

Left: This client's hallway is a personal dressing area between her bathroom and walk-in closet. Inset: Drawer inserts and partitions increase organization. Right (two views): Closets that are visible from other rooms can be smart and pretty. A trompe l'oeil portrait of a client's dogs disguises a linen closet converted to sweater storage.

OVER-DOORWAY BOOKSHELVES

ELEVATION

SLANT TO MATCH
CEILING CONDITION →

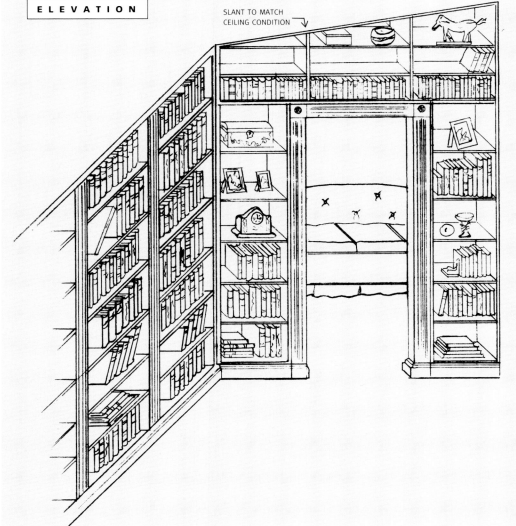

© Maxine Ordesky

Top: Too many books and not enough shelves? Expand your library into a hallway by lining the space with wrap-around, full-height shelves. Shallow shelves—the best kind for narrow passageways—offer sufficient storage for small books. Don't forget to cap the doorway. Bottom (two views): An elevated bookcase designed for a New York client isn't very deep, but it does add a great deal of storage space. Because it's adjacent to the apartment's front door, the ledge makes a nice staging area. Opposite page: Under-seat drawers could be cedar-lined for clothing or used for backyard toy storage.

© Jennifer Lévy/Maxine Ordesky, space design (both photos)

CHAPTER NINE

BASEMENTS AND ATTICS

Courtesy Velux-America Inc.

© Jennifer Lévy

Left: This converted attic playroom has good light and kid-size storage. Above: What's good for the roof line is good for the dresser. This custom sloped piece reclaims wasted space; the drawers utilize the wall's full storage potential.

Down and up and up and down we go in quest of storage space. Space to stow all the things we're sure our kids will want someday, room for everything our parents were sure we would someday want. Such is the life cycle of memorabilia. Invariably, our search takes us down to our basements—except in California, where there are no basements—or up to our attics. And do we find room in the dark, dingy tops and bottoms of our homes? Oh, yes, do we ever! So much room, in fact, that we pile in everything. And we're very likely never to see it again.

Conceivably, this is not the best way to preserve our most precious memories. Nor is it necessarily the most effective utilization of our basements and attics. But can we realistically slap a prohibition on attic and basement storage? No, we can't. Most of us need every square inch (or square centimeter)

of these spaces, but we can—and should—organize our attics and basements to their optimal potential.

OUT OF SIGHT, OUT OF MIND

Historically, homeowners underappreciated their basements and attics. These utilitarian rooms were like workhorses: reliable but unworthy of lavished attention. Why dress up a room no one sees? But suddenly, out of sight, out of mind became a good thing. Today, attics and basements are turning into home offices, bedrooms, and mini–health spas fit for royalty.

Deciding the future of your attic or basement, especially in storage-poor homes, requires a little fortune-telling. Peer as deeply as you can into your family's crystal ball and ask yourself a few questions. Namely, do you now need or foresee wanting your attic or basement as living space? If yes, will you require plumbing or gas lines? What type of access do you currently have to these levels? Is it safe and accessible to everyone who might use it?

If you opt for a finished living space, you're in for some major renovations, a discussion of which is best left to contractors, architects, and home-equity loan officers. I'm here to stress the importance of using your attic and basement at the very least for well-planned, organized storage.

ATTIC STORAGE: WHAT TO PUT WHERE

Madison Avenue imagines our attics as tiny treasure chests replete with rocking chair, trunk, and antique full-length mirror for modeling Grandma and Grandpa's finery. It's a romantic, if not altogether realistic notion. Fortunately, in an organized attic, there's room for Madison Avenue and reality.

Don't let trash spoil your treasures. Reserve your attic for memorabilia, not junk. Distinguish between nostalgia and stuff you're saving just in case it might be worth something someday—baseball cards and comic books excepted! (I still dream about the first-edition comic books my mother threw away.) Now organize. Group your belongings categorically, either by family member, by use, by age, by origin, or whatever makes sense for you. Label every box and keep an inventory and location list elsewhere in the house; it'll save trips up and down stairs when Neighbor Jane comes knocking, asking about your extra crock pot.

ATTIC STORAGE: SPACE-SPECIFIC SOLUTIONS

Fit the storage to the place. Purchase or build shelves or bookcases sized to fit along the knee wall, the short wall beneath your attic's sloping roof. You can buy perfectly adequate, inexpensive units at local home-improvement centers or commission a carpenter to build exactly what you need. Other attic storage solutions include these suggestions.

1 Hanging shelves from the collar beam (see drawing below).

2 Nailing shelves between the exposed studs.

3 Converting the space between the rafters to

HANGING SHELVES FROM COLLAR BEAM

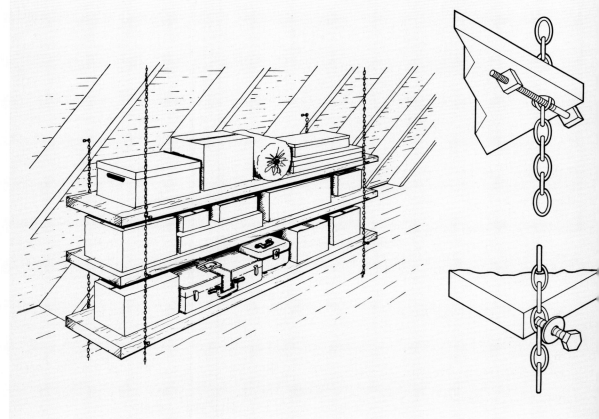

In an unfinished attic, hanging shelves (securely anchored at top and bottom) increase storage and at the same time preserve your possessions in a visible, accessible manner. Shelves also keep valuable mementos or records off the floor and away from pests. Remember, each shelf needs to be bolted or otherwise attached to the chain.

© Eric Roth/Gary Wolf, architect

a makeshift closet by installing poles or dowels between the rafters and hanging plastic-protected garments there.

4 Buying or building island-style storage in the attic. There's no traffic flow so it's okay to put something smack-dab in the middle of the room. You might use something you already own, pick up a retail display unit, or have something built.

5 Buying boxes from moving companies (for example, wardrobe boxes with poles, dish and book cartons, lamp-shade cartons, mirror and art boxes), labeling them, and stacking them categorically.

Let me say one thing to those doubting Thomases who question the wisdom of spending money to upgrade their attic's storage potential. Some investment in cabinetry and shelving, especially the knockdown variety, is money well spent. The very least you can do is make your attic a safe repository for your heritage if indeed that's where you're planning to store it.

BASEMENT STORAGE: LOOK OUT BELOW!

Beware of what you put at the bottom of your house, because it may stay there or, worse, perish there. Like attics, basements are obvious receptacles *d'objets* but not always well-designed ones. Packing away valuable mementos in the basement should be done with care. You'll want to guard against flooding, rodents, and your own memory loss. Be sure lighting is good so you can see where you put what. Of course, it helps to label boxes and to group them logically.

Like attics, several storage options work well downstairs. The best configuration is again perimeter and center. Place things along the walls first and then in the center of the basement. Reincarnate an old coffee or card table, for example, as a center island for basement storage.

Closed storage elevated off the floor is best, however, as it protects your things. You can buy or build what you need to outfit the basement's perimeter with storage units. Under the stairs you can do almost anything: build a closet, hang cabinets, buy rolling storage units.

If your attic is nonexistent and you have nowhere else to put things except in your basement, you could resort to loft-style storage. I say resort because I don't advocate loft storage. Even though lofts hold large, bulky items, these spaces are difficult to access, especially some of the makeshift basement storage lofts I've seen suspended from the first-story floor joists.

The curved ceiling of this converted attic is used as a backdrop for standard-height bookcases. Horizontal bookshelves nestle between vertical book-shelves. Decorated plywood panels factor in safety.

UNDER-STAIRS BINS AND SHELVES

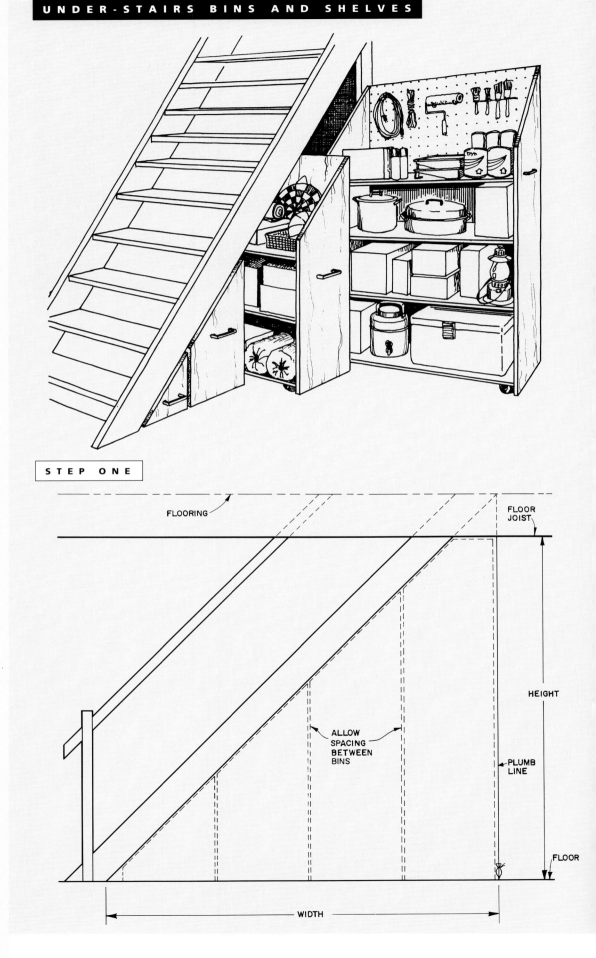

STEP ONE

FLOORING

FLOOR JOIST

HEIGHT

ALLOW SPACING BETWEEN BINS

PLUMB LINE

FLOOR

WIDTH

Right and opposite: Under-stair storage is often under-appreciated. Pull-out book-case-style units such as the ones depicted on these two pages, provide tremendous storage beneath basement—or kitchen—stairs.

From 50 Storage Ideas For the Home by Kate Armpriester and Mary Jane Favorite (all illustrations)

EXPLODED VIEW

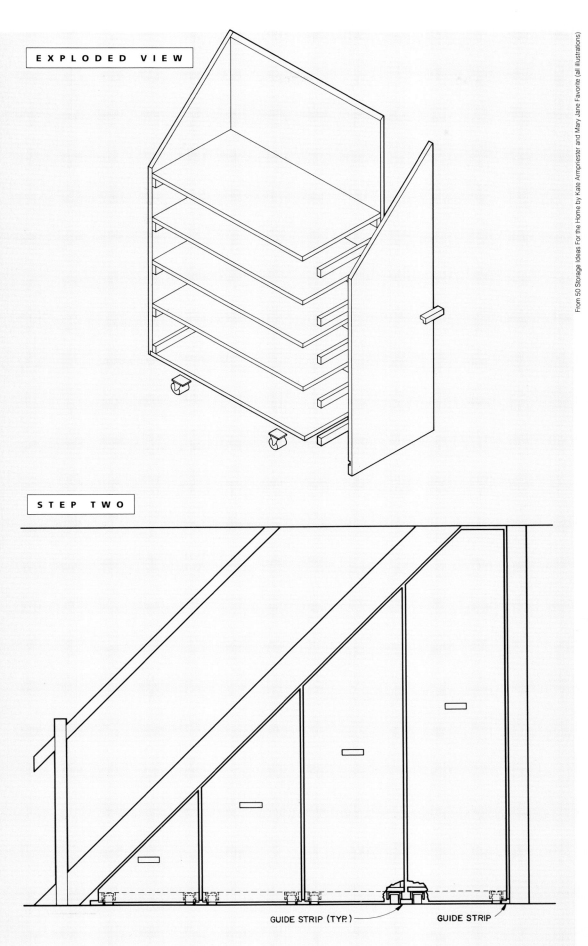

STEP TWO

GUIDE STRIP (TYP.) GUIDE STRIP

This particular design is good for several reasons: The units are on casters; they're simple and inexpensive to construct; and they hold a lot of stuff in an organized, accessible manner. What's not to like? For the construction competent, consider altering this design to include smaller shelves or even bins to serve various storage needs.

GARAGES AND GARDEN SHEDS

Left: Garages can be tremendously storage-intensive if properly organized, either by custom space planning or purchasing adjustable shelving components. Garage storage systems can be freestanding or wall-mounted and should provide both open and closed storage.

Your house doesn't have a basement, you dread the thought of wrestling boxes in and out of the attic, and your closets have given all they can in the battle for more space. If this is your storage nightmare, you've probably peered wistfully into your garage on more than one occasion, hoping for a miracle that would convert it into something more than, well, a garage. Believe it or not, you are that miracle. There's no reason why you can't organize your garage—or garden shed —as efficiently as any other part of your house.

THE BIGGEST CLOSET IN THE WORLD

Don't be intimidated by your garage. Think of it as a giant closet for your house. What your closet is to your bedroom, your garage is to your house: a place to put things. The trick, just like finding more space in your bedroom closet, is to approach the expansion challenge from a space-planning perspective. First, examine the current situation. Take inventory of what's already in the garage, the general layout, including roof design and height, and what types of activities take place there: pot-

ting and gardening, automotive and household repairs, or sewing and laundry, for example.

Second, throw out, recycle, or donate anything and everything you no longer need or use on a regular basis. I've said it before and I'll say it again: Purging is critical to planning efficient storage space. Do you really want to keep all of those old magazines? Studies show that 85 percent of all magazines and similar items that are filed away for future reference are never looked at again. Perhaps a local library would benefit from your collection.

By now you probably know the next step: Think about how you use your garage. Ask yourself some of the following questions.

1 Can the garage door be left open for extended periods?

2 What priority items must be stored in the garage?

3 Will there be a freezer or fridge in the garage?

4 Where are the light switches and electrical outlets?

5 What is the most convenient pathway into the house?

MINIMUM EFFORT FOR MAXIMUM STORAGE

Although additional organized storage space is alluring wherever it is, most people prefer not to spend a lot of time or money making room in their garages for more and more boxes. The least you can do to organize your garage and maximize storage space is to take advantage of readily available products and follow some basic organizing principles. Here are a few ideas and pictures to get you going.

1 Hang prefabricated or custom-made adjustable shelves on side and return walls.

2 If walls are unfinished, build shelves or cabinets between wall studs.

3 Stack storage crates in corners. Don't forget to label and date each one!

4 Stand prefabricated shelving units along walls.

5 Put pegboard or slat wall on walls for hanging storage.

6 Buy freestanding lockers to organize each family member's sporting equipment.

7 String a hammock along a wall to hold sports balls and lightweight items.

Courtesy Sporty's Tool Shop Catalog (all photos)

This assortment of retail items includes excellent, flexible solutions for storing and organizing the variety of tools and equipment cluttering many garages and garden sheds. Some would work equally well in laundry or sewing rooms.

GARAGE STORAGE

ELEVATION

ADJUSTABLE SHELVES
BEHIND DOORS

OPEN SHELF BELOW
CABINET

© Maxine Ordesky

TIP-OUT BINS — PULL-OUT TRAYS — DRAWERS

6 How much clearance do your cars need, including room to get in and out?

7 How many garbage cans do you require? Can they be stored outside the garage?

8 Are pests and/or vermin a problem?

9 Do young children or pets explore the garage?

10 Is there any room to expand the structure?

11 How frequently are you in the garage for an extended length of time?

FINDING SPACE IN THE GARAGE

Squeezing storage space out of your garage depends upon its size, shape, construction, and how much time and money you're willing to invest in the process. The most you can do is start from the ground up, building in storage space during construction. The least you can do is retrofit your garage with a few simple space-maximizing storage items and techniques. The first step is recognizing potential storage space in the garage.

Since cars consume the majority of garage floor space, walls and ceiling are the best solutions for lessening the storage burden on household closets and cupboards. Don't overlook the overhead space. You can suspend a loft or storage platform from ceiling rafters, assuming your roof is sloped and there's enough height to build the loft at least six and

a half or seven feet (1.98 or 2.1m) off the ground. To gain overhead storage in garages with flat roofs and, therefore, low ceilings, hang cabinets on the front wall just high enough to clear your car hood. Of course, you can always expand the garage.

If you're lucky enough to be in the construction phase—either adding on a garage or in the throes of building a whole new house—I think it's worth the extra money to make the garage structurally less like a garage and more like a room. Add a few extra square feet (or square meters) to accommodate a workbench or two and built-in storage units. In temperate climates, make room for a hobby corner, children's art area, laundry or sewing area. In the interest of being truly organized—and spending less time at the post office—you might also make space to store wrapping and packaging supplies. Insulate your garage enough to make it habitable and you'll be surprised how much more usable, organized space you'll add to your home.

EXPANDING YOUR EXISTING GARAGE

Short of building a new one, you might consider expanding your existing garage in one of the following four ways.

1 Knock down one wall and build out (assuming your roof line is already extended).

Designed for a client who enjoys gardening, this garage unit is jam-packed with shelf and drawer space.

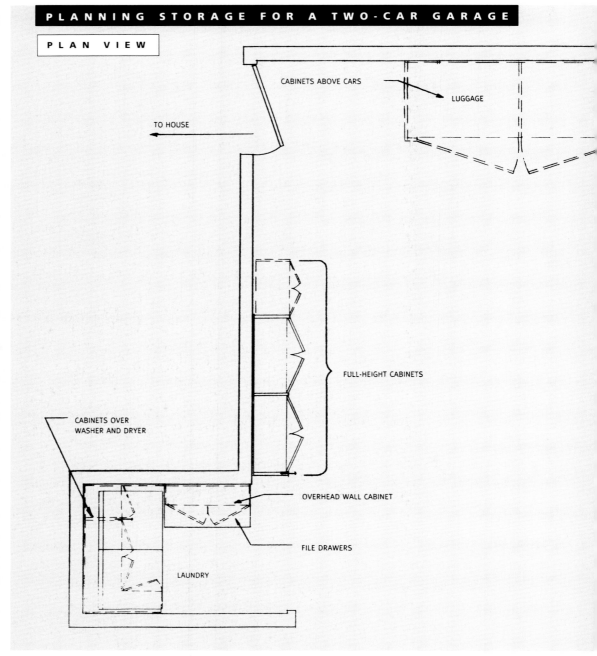

PLANNING STORAGE FOR A TWO-CAR GARAGE

PLAN VIEW

CABINETS ABOVE CARS

LUGGAGE

TO HOUSE

FULL-HEIGHT CABINETS

CABINETS OVER WASHER AND DRYER

OVERHEAD WALL CABINET

FILE DRAWERS

LAUNDRY

Right: Granted, most people don't space plan their garages to the extent I did for this client, but that's no reason not to take advantage of some of these smart storage ideas. We took advantage of an existing, empty alcove to design a mini-laundry room. The back-wall storage was sized and positioned to clear car hoods. The cabinets on the left side wall are appropriately shallow so they won't hinder movement in and out of cars. Cedar-lined closets were built on the right wall, and in the small return next to the house door, we added a small broom closet. In case you're wondering, all of the cabinetry was finished in gorgeous champagne-colored Formica.

2 Build out a section of one wall, making an alcove for activity or storage.

3 Build a storage unit on the exterior side of one wall and connect it to your garage with a doorway.

4 Add a storage shed or cabinet to an exterior wall.

These options vary in cost, but involve relatively little alteration to your existing structure. For space seekers without the stamina or stomach for major or minor home-improvement projects, follow the storage path of least resistance. Retrofit your garage. The sidebar on page 142 offers several suggestions.

GARDEN SHEDS

Picture-perfect gardens evoke a sense of romance, grace, even humility. To the admiring eye, they look almost effortless; pieces of quiet beauty for all to enjoy. Only the gardener sees behind Mother Nature's bucolic curtain. Fortunately for those of us without green thumbs, gardening enthusiasts claim to enjoy the toils of their pastime as much as its rewards. Fortunately for gardening enthusiasts, space planning is taking root in the garden shed.

In any home where gardening or landscaping is de rigueur, thought should be

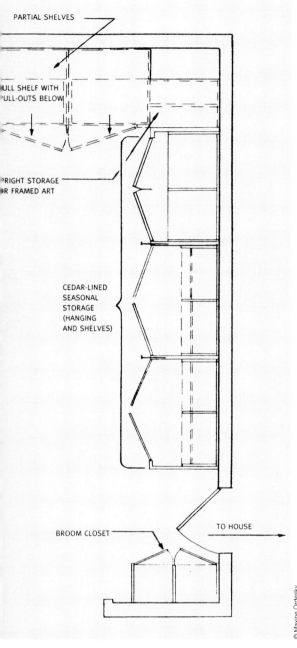

PARTIAL SHELVES

ULL SHELF WITH
'ULL-OUTS BELOW

PRIGHT STORAGE
R FRAMED ART

CEDAR-LINED
SEASONAL
STORAGE
(HANGING
AND SHELVES)

BROOM CLOSET   TO HOUSE

© Maxine Ordesky

© James Brett

Courtesy Williams-Sonoma

given to how and where necessary implements and supplies are stored. Our European ancestors took pride in their potting sheds, although some were considerably more stately structures than their name suggests. Modern-day garden sheds might be less grand—a small prefabricated hut or a sanctioned area of the garage—but are no less deserving with respect to space planning and organization.

THE NUTRIENTS OF ORGANIZED GARDENING

A garden shed of any size requires certain elements, namely a table or work surface, shelving or similar storage for tools and pots, large bins for soils, and ideally a sink or nearby water source. Proximity is key; the closer together you can store gardening essentials, the easier it will be to repot plants, mix soils, and tend to your garden. Of course, it's best to have a safe place to store sharp tools or harmful chemicals, preferably out of reach of children and pets.

The pictures shown on this and preceeding pages are only a sampling of the readily available items designed to make the activity of gardening a much more organized and enjoyable pastime.

Above: This pegboard creatively organizes shallow spaces and a special on-door hook holds tools. Left: I can't think of a more visual example of form following function than this lovely clay pot designed to organize garden hoses.

SPECIAL SPACE-PLANNING CONSIDERATIONS

SEASONAL STORAGE

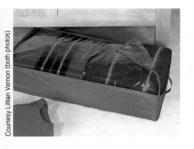

Left: No room to store off-season clothes? Look again. Durable garment bags come in all shapes, sizes, and patterns, just like our wardrobes! Above: Plastic storage bags sized to slip under beds make ideal storage for seasonal bedding.

For those lucky enough to be well endowed with closet space, Mother Nature poses little threat. But for the not so blessed who lack sufficient room in bedroom closets to store an entire year-round wardrobe, the change of seasons may induce "measured" anxiety. Whether you live in four-season country or in the temperate Sun Belt, you've experienced that weather-driven Kafkaesque metamorphosis that sends us scrambling to match our wardrobes with the thermometer.

Even Southern California's climate changes enough to warrant seasonal clothing. As a consummate organizer, I've developed some tricks to make the dreaded closet changeover less loathsome. Consequently, I use my limited closet and storage space much more efficiently and my clothes remain exceptionally well cared for.

READY, SET, SWITCH

In general, I find it easiest to retire no-longer-needed items as I stop wearing them. For example, once the weather gets too warm for gabardine slacks, I clean them and put them away rather than return them to my closet. However, you may prefer to change over your entire wardrobe at one time. If so, I suggest enlisting a little mechanical help in the form of a rolling, collapsible clothes rack. Use it to easily shuttle things between closets or to hold clothing neatly while you carefully lay to rest each seasonal item.

Whichever method you choose to switch your closets, always purge first! Get rid of anything—clothing, shoes, accessories—that offends your figure or your fashion sensibilities. Be brutally honest about streamlining your wardrobe. Why store a dress you didn't wear this season—or either of the last two seasons, for that matter? If it has value, give it to someone who will enjoy wearing it. Store away only what you'll want next season and donate the rest to charity.

Don't overlook the folded items in your drawers or on shelves. Move seasonal T-shirts, socks, night wear, and unmentionables to the front of the drawer or shelf if you have space. Finally, before you put away a season's worth of clothes, mend damaged items, resole worn shoes, and most important, clean *everything!*

Top: Even a collection of an-tique trunks can be designat-ed to hold seasonal storage. Remember to fold neatly. Above: This custom cabinet built for a New York client has a lift-up shelf above a deep space that's ideal for ski boots.

MAINTENANCE TIPS

Washing or dry-cleaning your clothes prior to long-term storage removes the odors that attract moths and other fabric-munching crit-ters. Moths feast on natural fibers. Wools and cashmeres are extremely vulnerable but cot-ton and linen make good eats, too. Dry clean-ing or laundering is especially beneficial because moths like soiled garments best. Which means, by the way, that you shouldn't be fooled by dry cleaners advertising *special* moth treatments at no charge. The reason there's no charge is because the prevention is inherent in the standard cleaning process!

Also, store your clothes in as airtight an environment as possible. Adult moths and their dining companions hate sunshine. Actually, brushing your clothes in the sun before storing them is a good way to get rid of any moths that may already be nesting in

your off-season garments. Additionally, use a moth preventive of some type. Because some people are sensitive or allergic to run-of-the-mill moth balls, stores do sell a variety of alternatives. Available in many shapes and formulations, these products offer scents such as pine, lavender, cedar, and herbs.

While I'm on the subject of moth preven-tives, let me caution you not to overdo it. How will you know? Well, if you notice a not-so-pleasant smell permeating your house the day after you've stored everything, you've used too many! You may have to air your clothes for a while before wearing them the following season.

Okay, your off-season wardrobe is clean and ready to be stored. What next? Space plan-ning, of course! In order to make room for sea-sonal storage, you can either *reconfigure* your existing storage space or *supplement* it.

FINDING THE SPACE

First, if you have adjustable poles and shelves in your closet, rearrange them to accommodate the upcoming season's clothes. Summer garments are made from thinner material and therefore require less hanging space than winter apparel. Lightweight sum-mer slacks can be folded over rather than hung long, because they don't crease as read-ily as do heavier slacks. Once the poles are correctly repositioned, adjust the shelves to suit your needs for the season.

Take advantage of closets with high ceil-ings. Installing an extra pole close to the ceil-ing allows you to hang all your off-season clothes out of the way, up at ceiling height. Conversely, if your closet provides only enough height for either the single obligatory pole and shelf or double-hung poles, then look down for extra storage. Assuming there's adequate clearance between your longest-hanging gar-ments and the floor, put your seasonal clothes in a box, suitcase, trunk, or other specially pur-chased storage unit and slide it away in that space. Of course you can also slide this type of storage under your bed.

Closets in other rooms, way-up-there top shelves, and awkward bottom drawers make great seasonal storage. Since you won't need to access those items for several months, it's fine to put them in hard-to-reach places. Another way to store seasonal items is in specially designed hanging closets. Available in retail stores or through many mail-order operations, these plastic garment bags generally measure fourteen inches (35.3cm) from side to side, twenty inches (50.8cm) front to back, and fifty to sixty-two inches (120 to 157.4cm) in length. They hold anywhere from ten to twenty garments on hangers, depending upon the thickness of the article. You can choose from patterned or solid designs, with or without see-through front panels. Some even come on casters for added mobility. I suggest buying the front-zipping styles.

These same sources also offer large box-like plastic containers for storing flat or folded items. When you pack clothes into these storage units, put a piece of tissue—or better yet, a dry cleaners' plastic bag—between (not over!) items to guard against wrinkles. Also from the retailers come items designed to increase your closet's vertical storage capacity. I don't recommend these for everyday use, however, and I will only grudgingly agree that they're okay for seasonal storage. There are several kinds, two of which may already be familiar to you. The first is the trapeze-style pole that suspends from your permanent closet poles, giving you a second pole below and twice the hanging room for short garments; the second device consists of multiple hangers that hook onto each other, one below the other. These allow you to hang several items vertically. Special space-saving hanging devices maximize your closet's vertical storage capacity without detracting from its overall horizontal space.

If worst comes to worst and you've resorted to plain old cardboard boxes for holding seasonal items, line each box with plastic. This will help keep air, moisture, and moths from damaging your clothes. The most important advice I can give you about box storage is to label each one! Additionally, note the number of boxes, the contents, and the location of each. Believe me, knowing what's where will save you oodles of time at the end of summer or winter, when you change your closet over to the upcoming season's wardrobe.

SAME SEASON, DIFFERENT YEAR

When you retrieve your items from seasonal storage, there are also certain things you should do to be sure your clothes remain in good shape. First, use the opportunity to thoroughly clean your empty closet. Vacuum nooks and crannies. Wipe down poles and shelves and spray them with a moth preventive. Next, as you unload, inspect every garment. Don't put away anything sporting loose buttons, ragged hems, or stains. (See why it's best to do all of this before you store your clothes?)

As you return items to your closet, think about where you're putting them. Start the season on the right foot. Arrange your wardrobe according to type of garment, color, frequency of use, or a combination of these systems. The goal is to make it easier for you to find what you want when you want it. I said it before and I'll say it again: space plan, space plan, space plan. Configure your closet to accommodate your clothes. Use your space efficiently and you'll be better poised to maintain your clothes and to enjoy them!

A few final cautions: Be careful not to put clothes that may bleed near white items. Trust me when I warn you not to hang a red suede jacket next to white slacks. Make room for delicate items so they're not crushed by other garments. Lastly, don't put dark-colored items in closet blind spots where lighting is poor. Likewise, hang lightly colored clothes away from windows and incoming daylight. And there you have it, a seasonal closet tailored for your wardrobe!

Courtesy Williams-Sonoma

This freestanding portable closet increases seasonal storage capacity with little effort or expense.

LINENS

Left: Space planning requires creativity. A traditional armoire can hold bedding and accent pillows as easily as a TV. Right: Vinyl-covered wire shelves make retrofitting a linen closet a rewarding do-it-yourself project.

When I talk about how to organize and store linens, I'm referring to bed sheets, comforters, duvet covers, pillows, towels, tablecloths, place mats, napkins, and napkin holders. Notice what's missing from this list: cleaning supplies, small household appliances, coats, games, and boots. If for no other reason than to keep unpleasant odors from permeating your bed and table linens, try to resist the temptation to use your linen closet—no matter how small or large it may be—as an indoor garage.

In a perfect world, a two-story house would have a sizable linen closet on each level. In a slightly less than perfect world, a single-story house would have at least one big linen closet or two smaller ones so that table linens could be separated from bed and bath linens. In an imperfect world, where most of us live, we all need more space in however many linen closets we have.

BACK TO BASICS

Before discussing ways to make more space in your linen closet(s), humor me while I repeat some basic space-planning and organizing principles. First, get rid of linens you no longer use, including sheets for beds that you no longer have (a crib, for example). If you're hesitant to throw away your old towels when you buy new, more fashionable ones, donate the outmoded towels to a charity or demote them to summer-camp duty. You could also designate them as drop cloths for future painting projects. Store old sheets and towels such as these in the inconvenient spaces of your closet or pack them in a box, suitcase, or trunk.

Second, measure your remaining inventory and determine how much storage space you need for each category of linens you plan to

One set of folded king-size sheets measures six to eight inches (15.2 to 20.3cm) high, ten inches (25cm) with a duvet cover. How you fold sheets or towels will greatly affect how much height they take up on a shelf and determine how much shelf space is used. It's best if you fold all linens or towels stored on the same shelf in the same manner. Consistency may be obsessive but it pays high space dividends.

You know I'm fond of using dowels to hold ties or scarves, but in linen closets, they're a smart way to store towels, bulky blankets, or tablecloths. Because they're attached to walls or (solid) doors, dowels offer visibility and the added benefit of clearing shelf space. A collection of colorful quilts hung on dowels can organize and brighten the bedroom. These construction views give you an idea of how this particular design is built.

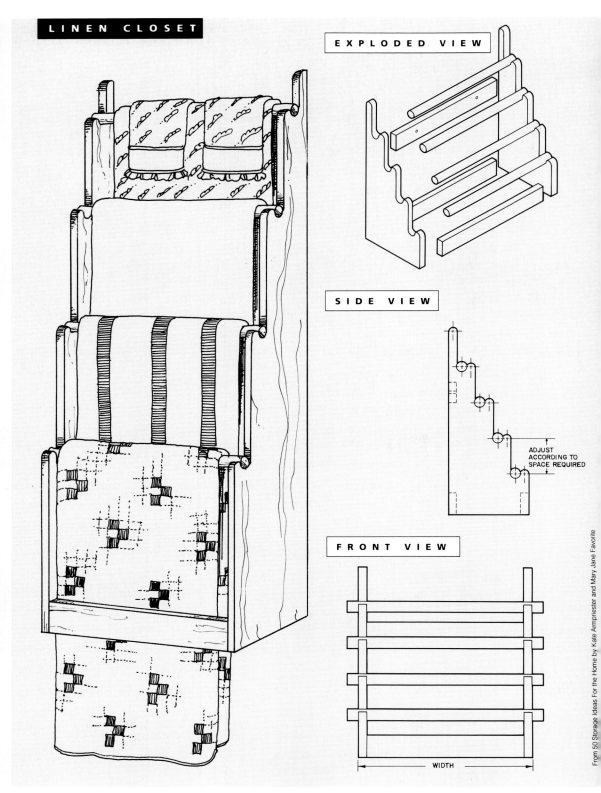

LINEN CLOSET

EXPLODED VIEW

SIDE VIEW

ADJUST ACCORDING TO SPACE REQUIRED

FRONT VIEW

WIDTH

From 50 Storage Ideas For the Home by Kate Armpriester and Mary Jane Favorite

store in the closet. Experiment with different folding techniques. The best finished shape—rectangular or square—is whichever one fits most economically on your shelf configuration.

Practice the "proximity principle": Place your linens as near as possible to where you use them. If you have the space to keep towels in each bathroom, you'll have more room in your linen closet for *all* of your bedding, even seasonal items. Similarly, consider keeping place mats and napkins in the dining room or in a kitchen drawer.

IN SEARCH OF SHELVING

The most basic way to get more shelf space in your linen closet is to add more shelves in one of two places. Shelves in a standard linen closet can be as much as sixteen inches (40.6cm) apart in height. That's ample room to build a half shelf for holding small hand towels, washcloths, or napkins. You can also hang plastic-covered wire shelves or baskets under the upper shelves to generate storage from otherwise dead air. A second potential locale for additional shelves is on the side returns of your linen closet. If the returns measure six inches (15.2cm) or more, you can put up shelves there.

Hanging items that don't need to be folded is also a good way to free up shelf space. Tablecloths folded over hangers can be hung from hooks fastened to the closet's side walls or even on the door. Tablecloths can also be hung in a similar fashion to ties, in shallow wall cabinets fitted with dowels. By the way, dowel-style linen storage also works well in kitchen or dining room wall cabinets.

Courtesy Williams-Sonoma

LINEN CLOSET

ELEVATION

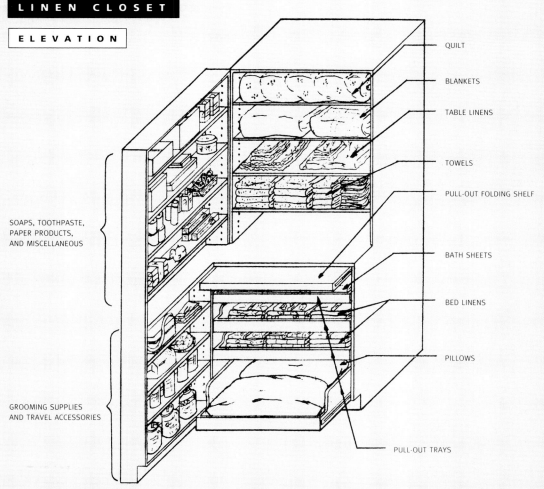

QUILT

BLANKETS

TABLE LINENS

TOWELS

PULL-OUT FOLDING SHELF

BATH SHEETS

BED LINENS

PILLOWS

PULL-OUT TRAYS

SOAPS, TOOTHPASTE, PAPER PRODUCTS, AND MISCELLANEOUS

GROOMING SUPPLIES AND TRAVEL ACCESSORIES

© Maxine Ordesky

Above: A readily available retail armoire with four adjustable shelves is outfitted with additional organizing accessories. This attractive stand-alone linen closet could provide flexible storage in any room of the house. Left: With five pull-out trays, twelve adjustable shelves, a pull-out folding shelf and a countertop, space planning turned this small closet into a dream linen closet.

CHAPTER THREE

SPORTING GEAR

Left: The necessity of space planning meets the fancy of art in a suspended bicycle. Right: This item-specific baseball rack will be functional only if hung within the young athlete's reach.

Sports and leisure activities are things we do for pleasure. The whole event, from gathering your equipment to putting it away, should be as enjoyable and effortless as possible. Sure, this is an appealing concept, but in many households, storing sporting equipment is an athletic event in and of itself. When you stop to think about how many different types—and sizes!—of sporting equipment there are and then multiply that by the number of sports each family member pursues, the storage challenge can be Olympic size!

Unfortunately, there is no one categorical way to deal with sporting equipment. The only common thread is that most types don't compact into smaller sizes (except for certain fishing rods and some camping gear) and that all equipment should be properly protected and maintained. Based on my experience, I think the best way to organize and store sporting equipment is to custom-build or buy specialized holders. The sidebar on the next page offers a few down-and-dirty tips.

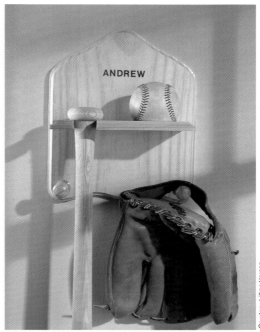

Courtesy Lillian Vernon

© Gary Quesada/Balthazar Korab Ltd (both photos)

SPACE VERSUS SPORTING EQUIPMENT: THE BATTLE FOR ORGANIZATION

Round 1: Pick a venue. Popular sites include garages, basements, attics (for seasonal gear), bedroom closets, mudrooms, laundry rooms, spare closets, and all of the above. Try to keep items that may be dirty, ski boots, athletic shoes, or riding boots for example, outside or away from main living areas. A footlocker in each athlete's bedroom will hold most sporting equipment. To really get in the spirit of the game, install several lockers in a corner of the garage or basement.

Round 2: Establish a game plan. Keep everything related to the same sport in the same place. Clock management is essential in any sport; save yourself time and energy searching for tennis balls by keeping them with the tennis rackets.

Round 3: Execute perfectly. Supplement your storage skills like a pro. Learn to use specially designed storage items and devise an organization system that is easy to follow.

Round 4: Team play. Enlist full cooperation from all players. Each person should be responsible for organizing his or her own sporting equipment.

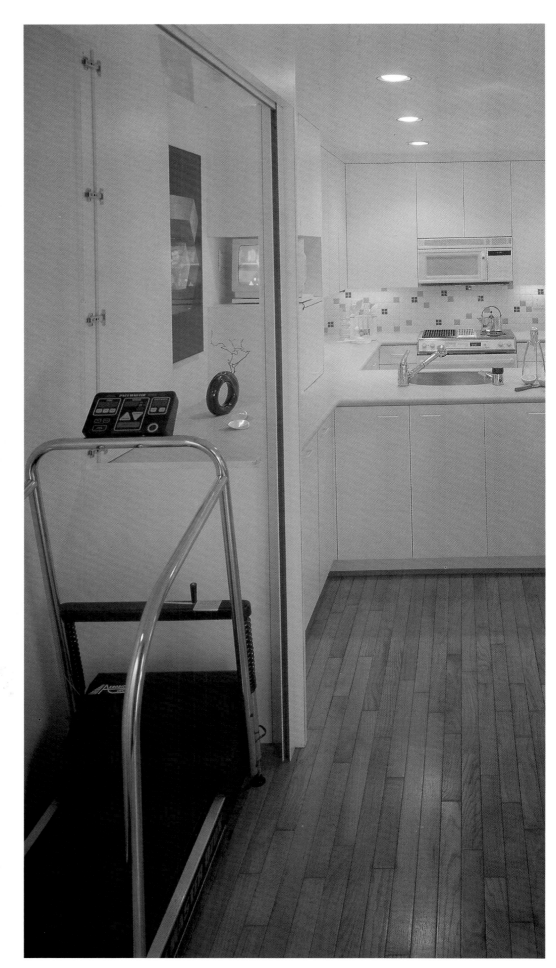

Courtesy Racor, Inc. (all photos)

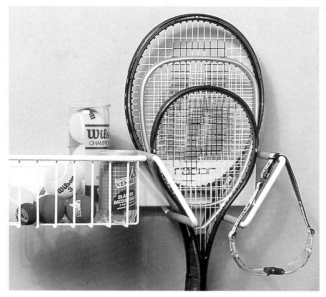

Opposite (two views): Diet inspiration is only a treadmill away. Whether custombuilt or converted from an existing wall closet, this tiny kitchen garage is a clever solution for storing a bulky piece of exercise equipment. This page: Many types of sporting gear can be stored off the floor in special caddies that securely hold related items in one place. Hang sporting equipment caddies in garages or mudrooms.

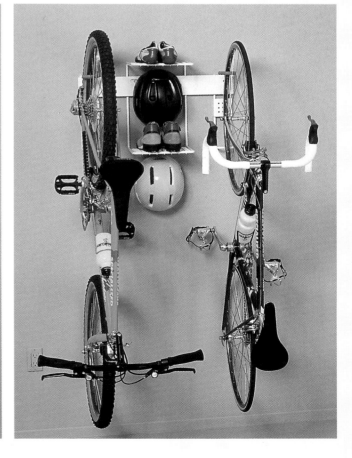

Courtesy Exposures, Inc.

© Michael Garland/courtesy Home Magazine/manufacturing by Wilson Art

© Jennifer Lévy

CHAPTER FOUR

PHOTOGRAPHS

Left, counterclockwise from top: Good space planning allows room for displaying family treasures in heirloom frames; on a personal, changing gallery ledge; pressed into diaries; or in boxes that also organize negatives.

Courtesy Lillian Vernon

When I was a young mother of two, I had a friend who was busy with eighteen-month-old twins and a newborn. As our children grew, we both took lots and lots of pictures. I labeled and placed my photos into albums as soon as they were developed. My friend insisted she would organize her pictures when her kids went to kindergarten. At least then she would have mornings to herself. She finally started her picture project after her three children graduated from college.

The consequence of this kind of procrastination is that you forget dates, events tend to become blurred, and you lose the opportunity to share the pictures over the years with family and friends. Don't wait to organize photos until you can savor the process; just think of all the moments your children lost that could have been spent reminiscing or glimpsing relatives never even met.

Decide on a method, and keep it simple! As in any organizing methodology, the more complicated or time-consuming, the less likely you are to follow through. Some people prefer to keep all their pictures chronologically. I prefer this method and like to display some shots from each roll of film as it's developed. By putting a few favorite shots on a family bulletin board, everyone can enjoy the most current pictures. Of course, I label the ones I don't display and put them immediately into a photo album. I leave the negatives in the envelope, label it with the date, event, or other identifiers, and note which album the photos are in. I then file the envelope chronologically in a box along with the other negative envelopes.

Envelope storage is also the simplest, least expensive way to organize the photos if you can't take the time to put each one into a photo album.

ORGANIZED PHOTOS AT A GLANCE

I can't say enough about the value of a good photo storage system. Select specially designed boxes or albums; whichever style will best accommodate your pictures and store conveniently in your home. I prefer a simple three-ring binder because the photos are clearly displayed and I can quickly and easily add or rearrange photos just by inserting or moving pages. As in everything else, adjustability is best. I also suggest getting photo albums or boxes of uniform size to make storage easier. Stationery and photography supply stores usually offer a wide selection of photo-storage systems.

CHAPTER FIVE

CHILDREN'S ART SUPPLIES

Architect: Geri Kelley of Bauhs & Dring, Chicago, Il/Photo: Jessie Walker (both photos)

Left: This adventuresome, unique room utilizes vertical and horizontal space, which is important when space planning kids' rooms. Right: This custom bed frame has a pull-out desk with a durable surface and a pull-out aquarium. What a nice surprise!

Children's arts and crafts activities run counter to good organization. Finger paints, watercolors, markers, modeling clay, and glue should be used creatively rather than according to a prescribed methodology. Painting and pasting at preschool is one thing, but home-based arts and crafts have special problems. You want to protect your carpet and walls without stifling your child's creativity. A genuine puzzle. Don't worry, a little space planning will piece it together.

STUDIO 101

The goal is to organize the area where they'll pursue their creative endeavors without them knowing you've organized it. To begin with, arts and crafts should be limited to a specific area of the house, ideally a space that can be protected from your spirited van Goghs and where all their supplies can be safely stored. In other words, your child's art area should be a self-contained studio. It may seem farfetched, but your child's bathroom—if

CREATING ROOM FOR CREATIVITY

Children's artistic adventures can be messy and potentially harmful. Keep these key points in mind in the interest of establishing a safe and organized creative environment.

■ Check all labels; buy only water-soluble art products.

■ Do outside what can be done outside. Let your children do their finger painting on the porch or patio on nice days. They'll have plenty of inspiration, and you won't risk interior stains.

■ Buy art toys designed to hold their supplies, such as easels with containers for paints and brushes.

■ An arts-and-crafts table in a child's room—even a folding card table—could be the beginnings of a desk and a good way to discipline them to work at a proper place.

■ Easels, chalkboards, erasable bulletin boards, crayons, and blank newsprint are good starting supplies. Some paint stores sell chalkboard paint, which you could use to turn part of your child's play area into an ever-changing canvas.

■ You can make your own easy-to-clean finger paints. Mix some Ivory flakes with a little water until peaks form and then add powdered pigment to create the desired color.

■ If you give your child markers and crayons, also provide him or her with proper places to use them. Lay in a supply of paper, preferably newsprint or a large roll such as those sold in art-supply stores.

Right, top and bottom: A paper towel–style dispenser and standard art supply caddy encourage young artists and teach good organizing habits.

it's large enough—is the perfect place for a beginner's art studio. Think about it. Bathroom surfaces are readily washable and your kids couldn't be closer to soap and water. If the bathroom is too small for a table, your kids can still work on the floor or on a board placed atop a sturdy open drawer or even the sink.

Other appropriate locations for a centralized art studio might be the kitchen or your child's bedroom. In either case, provide a table (with a durable, washable surface) and a cloth or mat to protect the floor. Again, keep supplies at hand. Paints, markers, and scissors can all be stored in colorful plastic bins or even decorated shoe boxes.

Courtesy Lillian Vernon

Courtesy Lillian Vernon

From 50 Storage Ideas For the Home by Kate Armpriester and Mary Jane Favorite (all illustrations

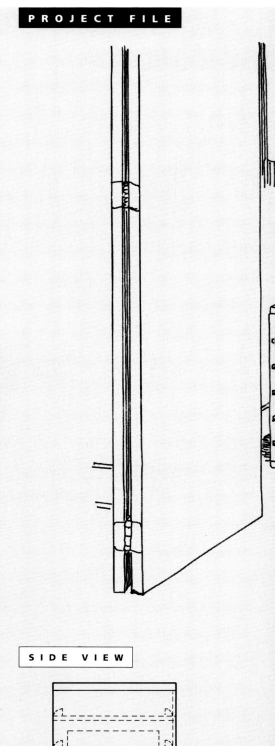

SIDE VIEW

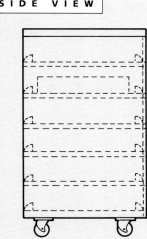

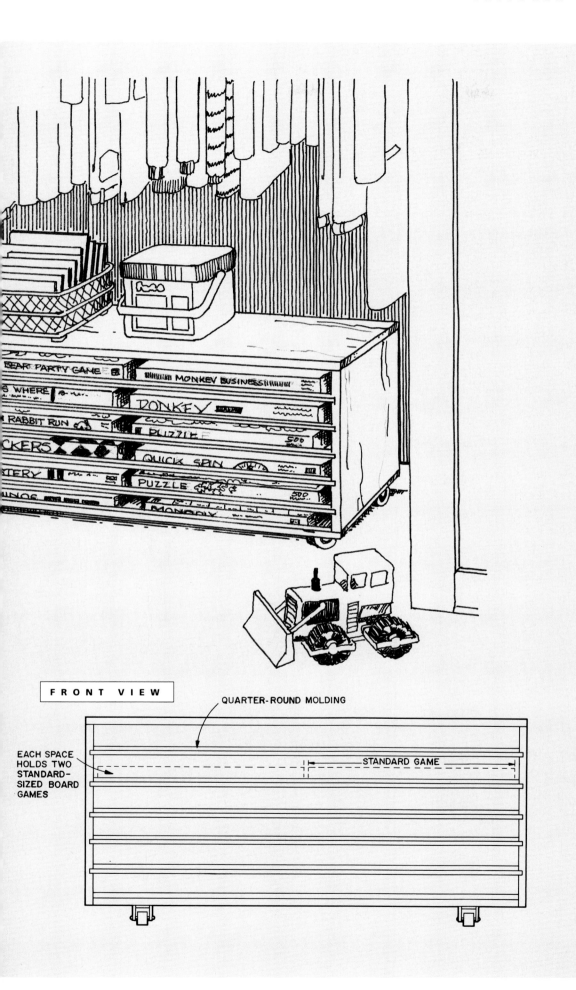

FRONT VIEW

QUARTER-ROUND MOLDING

EACH SPACE
HOLDS TWO
STANDARD-
SIZED BOARD
GAMES

STANDARD GAME

Left: Oh, the games children play! Why does everything seem to end up everywhere except where it belongs, with favorite playing pieces lost forever? Perhaps it's because the proper storage area is too cluttered or too difficult for your kids to access quickly. Put an end to toppling boxes and sprawling game pieces with this organized game file. Patterned after the flat drawers used by architects and artists for holding large drawings, this portable unit has individual shelves for several games. Kids simply slide boxes away when they finish playing. It makes space-planning sense because it rolls away into a closet or a family room corner. P.S. The top doubles as storage or a playing surface. This game file might help adults clean up faster, too!

CHAPTER SIX

VALUABLES

Left: This client wanted to store her jewelry collection in a concealed, locked manner that would still present the pieces in a particular fashion. My design for this custom cabinet features thirteen drawers that are lined with synthetic suede — to hold the items in place— and sized for various categories of jewelry. Right: Fitted for hanging files and shelf space, this freestanding safe also has a safe within a safe for passport-size documents.

Courtesy Sporty's Preferred Living Catalog

By definition, a valuable is something of exceptional worth, either monetary, personal, or legal. Our most precious valuables—photo albums, home videos, and personal keepsakes—cannot be replaced if lost or damaged. I wish I could tell you how to protect these mementos from theft or destruction, but short of locking them away in a hidden safe, I don't have many tips. What I want to do in this section is offer some advice about storing other valuables—cash, jewelry, and important documents—from a space-planning perspective.

Like any organizing project, the first step is to take inventory, noting how much secure space your valuables require. Some valuables you may want at home, while you may feel more secure storing others in a bank safe-deposit box. Of the former, you may want some to be concealed but easily accessible and others to be kept in a hidden safe at all times. (Stock certificates, wills, or real estate deeds could be kept in a safe-deposit box or at a lawyer's office.) If you're comfortable merely concealing your valuables, the sidebar on the next page will give you some ideas. Those of you who want more information about making room for home safes, take a look at Lesson 1.

CONCEALED IN PLAIN SIGHT

If you keep expensive jewelry or extra cash lying around for any fool to see, any fool will....The trick is to fool the pro. Although I'm hesitant to reveal my favorite concealment tactics, I will share some good ones.

The Kleenex camouflage: Carefully pry open one end of a tissue box and remove some tissues from the center. Place your jewelry roll or cash envelope in between the remaining tissues and reseal the box with double stick tape. Put the tissue box back at the bottom of the supply stack and no one will be any wiser. Hint: Keep the box in your bathroom and away from unsuspecting spouses or children who may hastily grab the first available tissue box in a moment of need.

Portable protection: Hanger covers with hidden pockets guard your valuables at home and on the road.

Cold dough: My mother-in-law used to wrap large bills in tin foil and freeze them right along with the brisket and coffee cakes.

Can it: The concept of hiding valuables among household supplies is a time-honored tradition. I know plenty of people who stash their cash in ordinary-looking groceries and bury the item in a large pantry or at the back of a very deep shelf. The idea here is to make it as difficult as possible for a would-be thief to find and raid the one container with your valuables.

Faux bottoms: Piano benches, hassocks, vanity stools, and decorative benches are all ideal pieces of furniture for hiding valuables beneath a false bottom. Any seat that lifts is a worthy candidate. Even things that pull out, say a deep bathroom drawer, could have a false back with a hidden section that remains out of sight unless a lever is released. A bathroom hamper with a false bottom is another hiding place that's easy for you to access but too time-consuming (not to mention smelly!) for a thief to bother investigating. The more your faux bottom furniture complements your decorating, the more effective the hiding spot.

Toe-kicks: Build touch-latch drawers into the recessed toe-kick of bathroom or closet cabinetry. These spots make good shallow hiding places. If built well, they blend beautifully with the cabinetry. One caution: Toe-kicks require careful construction for them to function right.

LESSON 1: FINDING SPACE FOR A SAFE

Be realistic about where you're going to put your safe and how much construction may be involved. There are two basic types of safes available: burglarproof and fireproof. Burglarproof safes should rest comfortably on a fixed shelf and be bolted down to the shelf or to a side wall so they can't be hauled off. Fireproof safes, on the other hand, often require structural reinforcements to support their extra weight and should not be bolted down because cutting any type of a hole into the safe will compromise its fire-retardant qualities. In my opinion, both types should be installed at eye level, but keep in mind that building a safe into your wall involves construction because once the safe is inserted into the wall, the back end obviously needs to rest on something and be concealed. Wall safes work well when built into deep, custom-made cabinetry. If you're planning to frequently access your safe, don't buy a floor safe. In my opinion, they're too inconvenient.

LESSON 2: GETTING THE RIGHT DESIGN

Although only a locksmith or safe expert has the technical expertise to give you advice about which locking mechanisms are best, I can help you evaluate a safe's interior. My idea of a well-designed safe is one that holds your valuables in an organized, accessible manner. All safes should have some retrofitting. If you can't afford to commission custom partitions complete with pull-out acrylic palettes, at the very least invest in a few acrylic boxes or trays to organize your jewelry.

RETROFITTED SAFE

ELEVATION

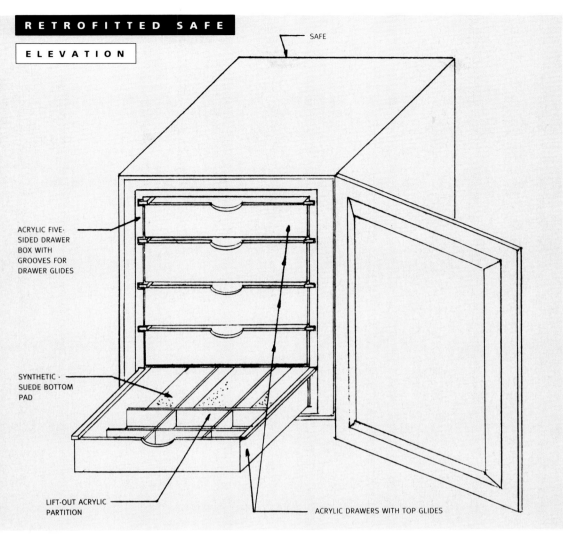

SAFE

ACRYLIC FIVE-SIDED DRAWER BOX WITH GROOVES FOR DRAWER GLIDES

SYNTHETIC-SUEDE BOTTOM PAD

LIFT-OUT ACRYLIC PARTITION

ACRYLIC DRAWERS WITH TOP GLIDES

CONCEALED SECTION BEHIND DRAWER

DETAIL

CONCEALED SECTION

LEVER STOPS

TOP DRAWER

PUSH/PULL LEVER ATTACHED TO UNDERSIDE OF COUNTER

BANK OF DRAWERS

ADJACENT KNEEHOLE OR ACCESS SPACE

© Maxine Ordesky (both illustrations)

Opposite: Though not new, these three techniques for concealing small valuables make good sense. The faux book and cans are easily hidden among real books and household supplies, and the safe requires minimal installation construction because it fits between the studs. This page, top: Space planning knows no limits. Retrofitting a safe interior with custom, movable trays, as illustrated in this drawing, provides better access to valuables. Bottom: A false back in this custom-designed drawer creates a concealed compartment that's ideal for hiding items.

CHAPTER SEVEN

COLLECTIONS

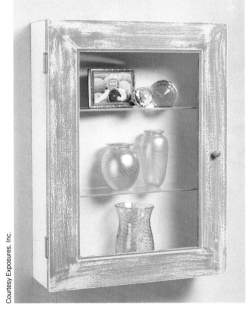

© Michael Garland/design by Andy & Yvonne Newman

Courtesy Exposures, Inc.

Left: Talk about your plate rail. Shallow shelves form an unobtrusive display space for this extensive collection of country tableware. Above: A small wall-hung vitrine protects fragile items. Right: Cigar-box storage revisited...and dressed up.

As I started to think about all the different ways to store and organize collections, I naturally recalled the myriad collections encountered in my friends' and clients' homes. Believe me, there are as many things to collect as there are people who collect them. Just for fun, take a quick look at the sampling below. How many of these things are on your shelves?

■ Antique eyeglasses ■ Hats ■ Antique kitchenware or tableware ■ Matchbooks ■ Baseball or sport cards ■ Model trains, planes, automobiles ■ Baskets ■ Pill or snuff boxes ■ Books ■ Pipes ■ Cake or candy molds ■ Pitchers ■ Cameras ■ Ribbons and trophies ■ Candlesticks ■ Spoons ■ Christmas ornaments ■ Stamps ■ Coins ■ Teapots ■ Decorative glass ■ Teddy bears, stuffed animals ■ Dolls ■ Thimbles ■ Figurines ■ Toy soldiers

Some of these items are purely decorative, others are also functional. How you organize your collection depends upon how you define it: for display only or for display and occasional use. If you collect valuable antique candy jars, you'll probably feel more comfortable protecting your treasures behind glass. If, however, you prefer your collection to be used as well as seen, you'll have different space-planning decisions to make. The size of your collection also matters. Forty or fifty porcelain snuff boxes could easily decorate tabletops throughout your home; a half dozen Indian ceremonial headdresses should probably hang together on one wall in one room. Finally, you also have to consider how much protection your collection needs from incoming sunlight, circulating air, and dust.

Courtesy Exposures, Inc.

COLLECTIVE STORAGE SPACE

Just like sporting equipment, there's no one way to organize and store all collections. Some of the ideas presented below may seem like common sense, but you'd be surprised how easily people overlook obvious ideas when they're scrambling for more space.

- Baskets
- Bookshelves
- China cabinets
- Collage boxes, framed and hung or resting on a table
- Cup and saucer holders
- Curio cabinets
- Custom-built wall units or free-standing cabinets
- Freestanding pedestals (if hollow, they can also contain storage space)
- Glass-fronted kitchen or dining cabinets
- Plate rails
- Plexiglas cubes placed on shelves or tables
- Slat wall
- Tabletops
- Vitrines
- Wall-hung glass or mirrored display shelves

Above right: Dividing this custom display case into different-size cubbies gives each art piece due prominence. Right: Like collectibles, vitrines come in all sizes and styles. Choose one to complement your collection and optimize display space.

© Michael Garland/design by Alice Fellows

In general, I recommend storing and displaying functional collections in the room where they might be used—hand-painted dinner plates in the dining room or kitchen, for example. It is preferable to store collectibles such as stamps or coins in specially purchased storage containers. That way your collection will be organized and safe. Of course you still have to make room to store the book or box, but that shouldn't be too diffi-

Courtesy Lillian Vernon

cult given everything you've already learned about space planning! In dealing with small, decorative items, mirrored units with ample lighting are nice because they allow you to enjoy your favorite pieces from all angles. If the elements of your collection vary drastically in size and shape, you're best off buying or building storage with adjustable shelves.

CHILDREN'S COLLECTIONS

Kids save the darnedest things. About the only collection that won't tack neatly on a child's bulletin board or rest on a dresser are those tiny amphibious creatures they sneak home in their pockets. Assuming you have your own policy for dealing with amphibians, here are few ideas to help your child organize their inanimate belongings.

Because kids like to put things on their walls, you can try "upholstering" a wall with self-adhesive corkboard. You can also use burlap or grass cloth stretched over a wood frame. If your little boy saves baseball hats, why not stop at a display house and pick up a few Styrofoam heads to make the display more fun. Your kids might even have fun drawing faces on them. Display houses (see sources at the back of the book) in general

© Bruce Katz/Jane E. Treacy & Larysa B. Kurylas, architects

are a good source for items such as Plexiglas cubes to organize and hold collections of all shapes and sizes. Pegboard or slat wall is another clever way of organizing a collection. Again, these are flexible display systems, which makes them particularly attractive to older kids and teenagers, whose notions of what's worth saving change rather quickly.

If your child collects a lot of different things, you should collect boxes of all kinds—cigar, shoe, hat, or acrylic—for extra storage. As long as a box is rigid and has a top that opens and closes well, it's a prime candidate for organizing all the tiny things kids save.

Courtesy Exposures, Inc.

Above left: The ultimate in collection storage—custom, floor-to-ceiling, built-in display cases with adjustable hole-and-peg glass shelves and accent lighting. Left: Memory boxes preserve items that are otherwise difficult to display.

CHAPTER EIGHT

WINE

Courtesy Williams-Sonoma

© Michael Garland/design by Lauren Dorf

Left: A wine enthusiast cultivates a collection in this well-planned wine-tasting room, complete with open and closed storage. Right: Store wine anywhere. These honeycomb wine bins fit into wide and flat spaces as well as tall, narrow cabinets.

I think the most important—and universal— consideration for storing wine is the environment. Wine is best stored at a consistent temperature. Expert consensus is 55°F (12°C), although some support variances as much as twenty degrees, depending upon the type of wine. Humidity in the storage area should remain at approximately 60 percent. Dry air can cause the cork to shrink, allowing air into the bottle. For this same reason, wine should be stored horizontally and slightly slanted so the cork stays moist. Beyond these important conditions, the only other determining factors in storing wine are the quantity you plan to buy and how much space you have to store it.

Space planning for wine storage depends upon your commitment to collecting. Do you keep a few bottles around for occasional enjoyment? Do you stock a dozen or so cases of the same vintage? Do you own valuable, rare wines? How frequently do you draw from your collection? For small collections, it's a good idea to investigate retail wine holders and coolers.

If you don't have the space to buy or build specialized wine storage, even for a small or moderate collection, honeycomb-style wine-bottle holders called The Wine Hive®

Courtesy Sporty's Preferred Living Catalog/Siematic kitchen

VINTAGE TIPS

1 Store wines by category—reds, whites, desserts, aperitifs—so you don't have to search for the desired bottle.

2 Catalog your collection, noting the date at which the wine should be consumed. Use index cards (or a computer) so you can easily update your catalog.

3 Organize the catalog by wine type and by expiration date so you can fully enjoy your collection at its prime.

These small, commercial-style refrigerators turn a kitchen island into a convenient wine or champagne cooler. The island itself is notable for the drawers—sized specifically for their contents—and wraparound towel bar.

enable you to store your collection in the necessary horizontal position. This particular wine-bottle holder allows you to stack your wine bottles securely on any shelf in any cabinet. You can make the stack as wide or as high as the space will allow. True adjustability!

For adamant collectors with space to dedicate to wine storage, a wine cellar is the ultimate storage system. You can buy prefabricated, self-contained wine cellars in a variety of sizes and styles. All you need to do is plug

them in and adjust the temperature and humidity controls. True connoisseurs, however, will want to custom-design a storage area for their collection. You might even want to include a table for making notes, a cataloging system, a drawer or cabinet to hold implements, and a decanting area. It's also nice to keep a basket or something nearby for smoothly transporting unopened bottles to the dinner table without disturbing the sediment in the bottle.

© Phillip H. Ennis

Courtesy Wood-Mode

© Jennifer Lévy

Three different spaces, three different collections, three wine-storage solutions. Above: Diagonal bins for volume. Far left: Cubbies for divided storage. Left: Custom pull-out for a few favorite bottles.

CHAPTER NINE

SEWING

Designer: Anna Meyers Interiors, Ltd., Chicago, Il/Photo: Jessie Walker

Courtesy Ikea

Left: Space planning is about personal preference. In rooms where visibility inspires creativity, open shelving can be an organized storage alternative to drawers. Above: This compact sewing center is an adjustable wall-mounted retail system that makes excellent use of a corner.

Sewing is definitely not my forte; just threading a needle ranks as a notable achievement. While I admit I'm no seamstress, I have space-planned sewing rooms and areas for several clients who are more graceful than I with needle and thread. In addition to the ideas and pictures presented on the following pages, notion and sewing supply stores or mail-order houses may also have good space-saving organizers for ardent seamstresses and tailors. You might even take your storage cues from the retail display items.

SEWING MACHINES

A portable sewing machine with cover and handles takes up very little space and can be easily stashed in a closet. The sewing machine that retracts into a self-contained cabinet takes up more floor space but allows you to use the surface of the cabinet as work space. Another advantage to machines that are built into their own cabinets is that they offer at-hand storage for bobbins, threads, and extra needles. If you're deliberating over what kind of machine to buy, keep in mind how often you expect to use it, where you will put it, and how many accessories you'll need to keep at the ready.

Before going on, I'd be remiss if I didn't remind you that the best way to get space-efficient storage for your sewing machine and supplies is to commission a custom cabinet or table designed to hold your equipment and materials. A good space planner may even find and customize space in an existing cabinet or, better yet, give you a desk and a gift-wrapping area in addition to the sewing area.

STOWING YOUR SEWING

Organizing sewing supplies is the perfect time to unravel conventional storage ideas. For instance, you might use the same drawers architects have for protecting blueprints to store patterns or large pieces of delicate fabrics. Same-color buttons or bobbins fit neatly into baby-food jars. Here are some more item-specific storage ideas.

PATTERNS CAN BE STORED...
- Vertically, with bookends for support
- Vertically between plastic shelf dividers
- In file drawers
- On custom-made pull-out palettes in closets
- On door-mounted pantry-style shelves or racks
- In an old suitcase
- In divided magazine or pamphlet racks

STORE THREAD SPOOLS...
- On slanted drawer inserts, as spices are often stored
- On pegboard hanging on small hooks or pegs
- In custom-built drawers fitted with short pegs
- On a cabinet door, fitted with small shelves or pegs
- In plastic zip-lock bags for embroidery thread
- In plastic or acrylic drawer inserts

MATERIAL AND TRIM FIT NICELY...
- In custom-made pull-out trays or palettes
- In art-supply drawers designed to hold large drawings
- On custom-made dowels in a closet for holding bolts of fabric
- In an ordinary wall-hung shoe or jewelry caddy
- In an old suitcase
- In a revolving spice rack for small pieces or trims

TOOLS, PINS, NOTIONS CAN BE STORED...
- Hanging on pegboard
- In a small toolbox
- In a tackle box
- In acrylic drawer inserts
- In jewelry or toiletry caddies
- In a spice rack for pins or buttons
- In units that hold nails or screws
- In an outfitted sewing box

SEWING ROOM PLANS

PLAN VIEW

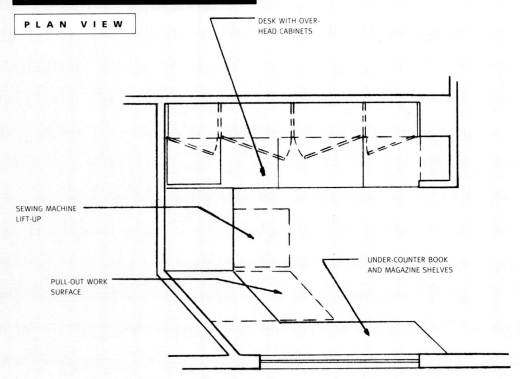

DESK WITH OVER-HEAD CABINETS

SEWING MACHINE LIFT-UP

PULL-OUT WORK SURFACE

UNDER-COUNTER BOOK AND MAGAZINE SHELVES

ELEVATION

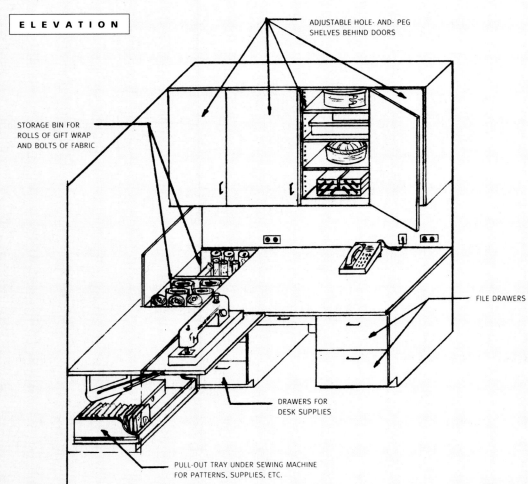

ADJUSTABLE HOLE- AND- PEG SHELVES BEHIND DOORS

STORAGE BIN FOR ROLLS OF GIFT WRAP AND BOLTS OF FABRIC

FILE DRAWERS

DRAWERS FOR DESK SUPPLIES

PULL-OUT TRAY UNDER SEWING MACHINE FOR PATTERNS, SUPPLIES, ETC.

© Maxine Ordesky

Courtesy Heller

Courtesy Heller

PATTERNS AND FABRICS AND THREADS, OH MY...

It's been my experience that people who sew also save. They collect odd buttons, material, trim, notions, and so on. These same people also have sizable pattern collections, a rainbow of threads and complementary bobbins, needles, and pins, not to mention specific types of cutting and measuring tools. Any and all time spent organizing these supplies will be repaid in more enjoyable sewing time. Try to avoid jamming everything into deep drawers. Ideally, all your materials should be visible and accessible. The sidebar on the opposite page lists several ways to organize sewing notions.

Opposite: This client needed a central workplace for her home office, sewing, and gift wrapping. The only available space was an alcove off her family room. I designed a pull-out, lift-up shelf for her sewing machine, a double-section bin for wrapping paper or rolled fabrics, and finally, a desk with file drawers and adjustable shelves above. Left: Store-bought containers on fixed shelves thread together an inexpensive yet organized sewing supply closet. Above: This plastic-coated grid has movable hooks for organizing sewing supplies.

CONCLUSION

Establishing a formula for staying organized is at best difficult. It's hard to realistically calculate the amount of time and energy you'll need. Nonetheless, the benefits of proper space planning and organization are immeasurable. In fact, space planning can enhance your life-style and environment at almost every phase of life.

THE SPACE-PLANNING CONTINUUM

Most young adults start out single, living alone or with roommates. Either way, most of today's young adults start their post-college life fully equipped with toasters, TVs, and furniture. When they marry, usually after several years of independent living and accumulation, two adults consolidate their two households into one. Time goes by, children enter the picture, and room has to be made for their clothes, furniture, toys, artwork, family photos, and videos, not to mention pets.

With children come guests...and grandparents who will no doubt want to stay with you rather than at a hotel so they can enjoy their grandchildren "every minute of the day." Along with the house and the kids comes the backyard, which begets lawn and garden equipment. Just when you mastered a way to organize the various sporting paraphernalia and summer-camp clothes, the kids are college bound. Don't get excited, though, this is only a temporary reprieve from the space crunch.

They'll still want you to store all their books and treasured memories until they have enough space of their own. After all, your basement and garage holds more than their tiny dorm room or apartment could ever store. Nevertheless, the house does slowly empty out again. But wait. After your children marry, they visit with their children. You'll need cribs, toys, safeguards—the whole kit and caboodle all over again.

Eventually, however, the time comes when your home is too big and you move into smaller accommodations. This stage, believe it or not, is the most crucial stage of the game for space planning. Squeezing a lifetime of possessions into a home that's one-third the size of where you lived before takes careful thought and planning. True, you'll probably pass many items on to your children to enjoy in their own homes, but you'll find that you'll be adding a few new items, too. When people retire they often

Here is the essence of space planning. Opposite: A carefully thought-out wall is functional, flexible, organized, easy to use, and pleasant to look at. Above: This bedroom configuration adapts to the room's slanted ceiling without compromising living space or storage.

Is your space sick? Heed the early-warning signs of dysfunctional space.

[1] Too many things are in one place.

[2] The wrong items are wedged into the wrong-size and -shape storage area.

[3] Items are stored horizontally when they should be standing vertically.

[4] Small items are obscured by larger ones.

[5] Adjustable space isn't adapted to fit your changed possessions.

[6] Frequently used items are out of reach.

bring their offices home, especially now that so many retirees remain active in their fields or pursue new endeavors.

Space planning allows you to control your space rather than the other way around. Too much control, however, can undermine your efforts. Don't overdo it. Symptoms of hyper-organization include spending too much time thinking about where to put things and needing too many supplies and gadgets to do so. Other indications that your space planning is becoming more dysfunctional than functional are in the sidebar at left.

THE METHOD BEHIND THE MADNESS

Space planning is to organization what discipline is to behavior modification: Without the former, it's difficult to achieve the latter. The idea behind space planning is setting everything up so that you can keep it organized. This is where the discipline comes in. To stay organized, you not only have to carefully plan

how to maximize your storage space but you also must take the time to keep your space working as it should.

Today's life-styles don't make this task any easier, especially if you're raising children. I've had many clients say to me that they just don't have the solitude they need to contemplate better uses of space. They put and place hurriedly, which only complicates the problem. I once read some very wise advice on the matter of Mom versus kids: Take your sails out of their wind. Discipline yourself to stay out of their routines at certain times. To work around my own children, I would occasionally retreat to my bedroom to make phone calls or write letters.

The other part of discipline is doing things when they should be done and doing them right. Don't throw something into the drawer mumbling, "I'll put it away later." Most professional organizers agree that papers should be handled only once and not shuffled between stacks of unattended notes. Following this rule

Right: When organizing your home, strike a workable balance between the space and your life-style. Be flexible. Two people could occupy this small workspace as easily as one thanks to an oversize desk and adjustable wall storage. Opposite: Good space planning begets good organization. This client's closet has just the right amount of space for his wardrobe and a center island.

© Peter Paige/Tony Antine, interior design

There is no "right way" to space-plan a cabinet, a room, or a house for that matter. An ingenious storage solution to one person may be impractical or unattractive to another. A professional space planner will help you assimilate your design sensibilities, life-style, storage capacity, and budget into usable, organized space. Here are some hints for hiring and working with a space planner.

Review the space planner's portfolio. Do you like what you see? Ask for letters of recommendation and talk to former clients. Be sure the candidate provides an understandable letter of agreement. This document should specify exactly what services (consultations, drawings, on-site follow-through) will be provided. The letter should also detail billing procedures. Finally, it's important that you chose someone with whom you feel a rapport. A professional space planner sees what's behind your closed doors; you must be comfortable with this.

To facilitate your working relationship, make a list of your needs, and note what you do and do not like about your current storage. Don't be embarrassed to mention something, regardless of how inconsequential it may seem to you. It's important that your space planner know as much as possible about any factors affecting how you use—or want to use—a space. Stick to your decisions. Changing materials or design can be very costly, both financially and spatially. If you're indecisive about what you want, you may not get something you can live with.

I start every space-planning job by consulting with the client for several hours. I then complete a detailed inventory of the possessions to be organized and thoroughly measure the existing space. Next, I propose plans for reconfiguring or reconstructing the space to meet the client's needs and budget. The drawings I present include building specifications, dimensions, and placement (what goes where in the new construction). Finally, I provide an exacting capacity comparison revealing how much space the client gained.

If you have a particularly challenging storage problem or are especially proud of a homegrown, inventive solution, please share! You may write me at Organized Designs, P.O. Box 6901, Beverly Hills, CA 90212-6901.

for possessions as well as paper generates less clutter. And clutter is something we could all do without. Let me give you an example.

During a lecture on space planning and organization when I was showing my audience how I managed to hold so many things in my tiny purse, one woman feverishly interrupted me. She pointed out that she carried a bigger bag so it would hold everything she might possibly need in an emergency—and added that my bag was much too small to hold mace. I asked her to show me the mace to see if I could indeed accommodate it. Well, she began rummaging through her bag...and rummaging...and rummaging until we were all laughing hysterically. If she had needed it in an emergency, she'd never have found it!

Staying organized is something you do every day of your life. Train yourself to think about your possessions. Stephanie Culp, author of several books on organization, including *How to Conquer Clutter,* stresses this point. "Evaluating whether you still use or need all of your possessions is always important but particularly so before relocating or remodeling. There's no point to beautifying your home only to move in among mountains of transplanted clutter."

Periodically question how well your space is planned: Can I reach it? Do I really need that where it is or could it go elsewhere? Can I see everything clearly enough? If your space is organized and functioning well, you will be, too.

SOURCES

The following list of sources includes individuals, stores, and companies that I've had contact with during my seventeen years in business. For businesses with multiple locations, I have listed the main office. For products sold through many different stores, I have named the manufacturer so that you may contact them directly for names and addresses of local retailers. Finally, the following sources are not comprehensive but are offered as a starting point and guide to products and services for organized storage in your home. Please note that extensive attempts were made to ensure the accuracy of the following names and addresses at press time.

CATALOGS AND/OR STORES

FOR GENERAL ORGANIZING AND STORAGE

Conrans Habitat
50 Main Street
White Plains, NY 10606
(914) 681-3400
Furniture, modular units, specialty items

Crate and Barrel
P.O. Box 9059
Wheeling, IL 60090
(800) 451-8217
Furniture, modular units, specialty items

Hammacher Schlemmer
2515 East 43rd Street
P.O. Box 182256
Chattanooga, TN 37422
(800) 543-3366
Specialty items

Hold Everything
P.O. Box 7807
San Francisco, CA 94120
(800) 421-2264
Assortment of home-storage and organizing items

IKEA USA, Inc.
1000 Center Drive
Elizabeth, NJ 07202
(909) 289-4488
Furniture, modular units

Lilian Vernon Corporation
Virginia Beach, VA 23479
(800) 285-5555
Assortment of home-storage and organizing items

Promises Kept
2525 Xenium Lane
P.O. Box 47368
Plymouth, MN 55447
(800) 989-3545
Collection of home-storage and organizing items

FOR CHILDREN

Hold Everything
(see Catalogs-General)

Lilian Vernon
(see Catalogs-General)

The Right Start Catalog
Right Start Plaza
5334 Sterling Center Drive
Westlake Village, CA 91361
(800) 548-8531
Some organizing and storage items

Toys To Grow On
P.O. Box 17
Long Beach, CA 90801
(800) 874-4242
Some organizing and storage items

FOR GARAGES AND SHEDS

Frontgate
396 Wards Corner Road
Suite 200
Loveland, OH 45140
(800) 626-6488
Organizing and storage items

Gardeners Eden
P.O. Box 7456
San Francisco, CA 94120
(800) 822-9600
Organizing and storage items

John Deere
1400 3rd Avenue
Moline, IL 61265
(800) 544-2122
Organizing and storage items

Solutions Inc.
P.O. Box 6878
Portland, OR 97228
(800) 342-9988
Organizing and storage items

Sporty's
Clermont County Airport
Batavia, OH 45103
(800) 543-8633
Organizing and storage items

FOR HOME OFFICES

Hello Direct
5884 Eden Park Place
San Jose, CA 95138
(800) 444-3556
Specialty items for use with telephones

Levenger
975 South Congress Avenue
Del Ray Beach, FL 33445
(800) 544-0880
Assortment of storage and functional accessories for books

Reliable Home Offices
P.O. Box 804117
Chicago, IL 60680
(800) 869-6000
Assortment of office and desk storage and organizing items

FOR KITCHENS

AristoKraft, Inc.
P.O. Box 420
Jasper, IN 47546
(812) 482-2527
Organizing and storage items

Colonial Garden Kitchens
340 Popular Street
Hanover, PA 17333
(800) 752-5552
Organizing and storage items

Crate & Barrel
(see Catalogs-General)

Crystal Cabinet
1100 Crystal Drive
Princeton, MN 55371
(612) 389-4187
Organizing and storage items

Hold Everything
(see Catalogs-General)

Kraftmaid
1422 Euclid Avenue
Cleveland, OH 44115
(800) 654-3008
Organizing and storage items

Lilian Vernon
(see Catalogs-General)

Williams-Sonoma
P.O. Box 7456
San Francisco, CA 94120
(800) 541-2233
Specialty kitchen items

FOR PHOTOGRAPHS, SLIDES, AND MEMORABILIA

Exposures
2800 Hoover Road
Stevens Point, WI 54481
(800) 222-4947
Organizing and storage items

FOR WINE

The Wine Enthusiast
Department W, 6
P.O. Box 39
Pleasantville, NY 10570
(800) 231-0100
Organizing and storage items

FURNITURE AND MODULAR STOR- AGE SYSTEMS

Conrans Habitat
(see Catalogs-General)

IKEA
(see Catalogs-General)

Plummer's International
8876 Venice Boulevard
Los Angeles, CA 90034
(310) 837-0138
Furniture and modular units for various rooms and functions

Rutt Custom Cabinetry
1564 Main Street
P.O. Box 129
Goodville, PA 17528
(215) 445-6751
Furniture and modular units for various rooms and functions

Workbench
470 Park Avenue South
New York, NY 10016
(212) 532-7900
Furniture and modular units for various rooms and functions

PRODUCTS

FOR CLOSETS

Acme Display
1057 South Olive Street
Los Angeles, CA 90015
(800) 959-5657
(213) 749-9191 in Los Angeles
A variety of hangers and other functional accessories

Compact Novelties
303 Fifth Avenue
New York, NY 10016
(212) 685-5830
Full line of wooden and other hangers, additional accessories

Guardian Products
P.O. Box 150357
San Rafael, CA 94915
(800) 334-0812
(415) 258-0701 in California
Fabric bags and other hanging items for organizing and storage

Hold Everything
(see Catalogs-General)

Lee/Rowan
6333 Etzel Avenue
St. Louis, MO 63133
(800) 325-6150
Closet products, including tie and belt racks

Lilian Vernon
(see Catalogs-General)

Loroman-Abott Industries
95-25 149th Street
Jamaica, NY 11435
(718) 291-0800
Ty-Master® tie and belt rack and organizing products

FOR GENERAL ORGANIZING AND STORAGE PRODUCTS

Elfa Corporation of America, Inc.
300-3A Route 17 South
Lodi, NJ 07644
(201) 777-1554
Vinyl-coated wire storage organizers for various rooms and functions

Grayline Housewares
1616 Berkley Street
Elgin, IL 60123
(708) 695-3900
Vinyl-covered wire organizing products for various rooms and functions

Racor
P.O. Box 2069
Portland, OR 97208
(206) 695-8599
Storage and organizing products for various rooms and functions

Rubbermaid Inc.
1147 Akron Road
Wooster, OH 44691
(216) 264-6464
Storage and organizing products for various rooms and functions

Stanley Hardware
480 Myrtle Street
New Britain, CT 06052
(203) 225-5111
Vinyl-covered wire storage systems for various rooms and functions

SPECIALTY HARDWARE AND BUILDING SUPPLIES

Constantine's
2050 Eastchester Road
Bronx, NY 10461
(800) 223-8087
Mail order source for tools and hardware for do-it-yourself construction projects

Hafele America
3901 Cheyenne Drive
P.O. Box 4000
Archdale, NC 27263
(919) 889-2322
Functional and decorative hardware, building supplies, and organizing items for various rooms and applications

Hafele Canada
6345 Netherhart Road
Unit 1-3
Mississauga, ONT. L5T 1B8
(416) 564-9830
Functional and decorative hardware, building supplies, and organizing items for various rooms and applications

Hardwood Veneer Association
5603 West Raymond Street
Suite O
Indianapolis, IN 46241
(317) 244-3311
Information and hardwood-veneer samples

Doug Mockett & Company
P.O. Box 3333
Manhattan Beach, CA 90266
(800) 523-1269 including Canada
Wire management systems (grommets) and other furniture components

Paul Associates
42-05 10th Street
Long Island City, NY 11101
(718) 784-2244
Decorative hardware and fixtures

Stor-A-Door
P.O. Box 1661
Darien, CT 06820
(203) 655-6786
Pocket doors and hardware

SPECIALTY PRODUCTS

Austin Chemical Company
10356 Christine Place
Chatsworth, CA 91311
(818) 360-1175
A neat, easy-to-use moth preventive

Black & Decker
6 Armstrong Road
Shelton, CT 06484
(203) 926-3000
Space-saving appliances

Cosmepak
P.O. Box 1907
Morristown, NJ 07962
(201) 993-9140
Bath and cosmetic organizers

Otis Elevator Company
2 Farm Springs
Farmington, CT 06134
(800) 233-6847
Dumb waiters and elevators

Plastic Mart
2101 Pico Boulevard
Santa Monica, CA 90405
(310) 451-1701
*Acrylic, custom-fabricated
ready-to-buy organizers and
drawer inserts for various
rooms and functions*

**Putnam Rolling Ladder
Company**
32 Howard Street
New York, NY 10013
(212) 226-5147
*Rolling and other style ladders
for various rooms and functions*

Rev-A-Shelf
2409 Plantside Drive
Jeffersontown, KY 40299
(800) 626-1126
*Retrofit items for cabinets and
pantries*

ARCHITECTS

**Marc Appleton, Ralph Mechur
Appleton Mechur & Associates**
220 Main Street
Venice, CA 90291
(310) 399-9386

**Duo Dickinson
Duo Dickinson, Architect**
94 Bradley Road
Madison, CT 06443

**James Estes
James Estes, Architect**
79 Thames Street
Newport, RI 02840
(401) 846-3336

**Robbin Hayne
Robbin Hayne, Architect**
6162 La Gloria Drive
Malibu, CA 90265
(310) 457-0732

**Harold Levitt
Harold Levitt & Associates**
221 North Robertson Boulevard
Beverly Hills, CA 90211
(213) 272-2280

**Richard Martin
Richard Martin Associates**
2102 Pontius Avenue
Los Angeles, CA 90025
(310) 477-3094

**Ronald McCoy
Ronald McCoy, Architect**
3221 Hutchison Avenue
Los Angeles, CA 90034
(310) 836-9087

**Robert Orr
Robert Orr & Associates**
Architect & Gardens
441 Chapel Street
New Haven, CT 06511
(203) 777-3387

**Don Swiers
Don Swiers, Architect**
11727 Barrington Court
Suite 203
Los Angeles, CA 90049
(310) 471-1711

**Jane E. Treacy
Jane E. Treacy, Architect**
1725 17th Street, NW
Washington D.C. 20009
(202) 234-4261

DESIGNERS AND PLANNERS

**Snuff Adams
L & S Interiors**
69-730 Highway 111
Suite 201B
Rancho Mirage, CA 92270
(619) 324-9413

**Joyce Bromiley
Bromiley Design Associates**
31346 Broad Beach Road
Malibu, CA 90265
(310) 457-4343

**Steve Chase
Steve Chase Associates**
P.O. Box 1610
Rancho Mirage, CA 92270
(619) 324-4602

**Susan Cohen
Susan Cohen Associates**
305 South Orlando Avenue
Los Angeles, CA 90048
(310) 828-4445

**Georgia Johnstone
Georgia Johnstone Designs**
1010-1012 North Hilldale
Los Angeles, CA 90069
(310) 276-3189

**Laurie Levitt
Barbara Treiman
Space Innovations Design
Group**
393 South Beverly Glen
Boulevard
Los Angeles, CA 90024
(310) 441-1688

**Linda London
Linda London Designs**
200 East 62nd Street
New York, NY 10021
(212) 751-5011

**Connie McCreight
Design Solutions**
556 South Fairfax Avenue
Los Angeles, CA 90036
(213) 939-2641

**Maxine Ordesky
Organized Designs**
P.O. Box 6901
Beverly Hills, CA 90212
(310) 277-0499

**Carol Poet
Poet Design Company**
540 N. San Vincente Boulevard
Los Angeles, CA 90048
(310) 652-9075

**Alanna Ponder
Alanna Ponder Interior
Architecture**
9348 Civic Center Drive
Suite 101
Beverly Hills, CA 90210
(310) 246-1966

**Gerry Saenz
Gerry Saenz Associates**
120 C Avenue
Coronado, CA 92118
(619) 435-7372

CABINETMAKERS

**Dan Crossey
Cotopaxi Woodworks**
2620 West Cucharras Street
Colorado Springs, CO 80904
(719) 635-5219

**John Agrios, Perry Hill
D & J Woodcraft Inc.**
3839 Hoke Avenue
Culver City, CA 90230
(213) 870-0377

**Eli Nadel
Eli's Cabinet Shop**
2732 Gilroy Street
Los Angeles, CA 90039
(213) 663-7817

**Michael Grubic
Grubic Cabinets**
2645 Abedul Street
La Costa, CA 92009
(619) 471-4727

**Ari Matsui
Ari Matsui Creative Woodworks**
1866 West 169th Street
Unit H
Gardena, CA 90247
(310) 516-7811

**Gary Schultz
Gary Schultz Custom Cabinets**
3515 Helms Avenue
Culver City, CA 90232
(310) 204-3407

**Julius Mann
Woodworking Inc.**
10-29 47th Road
Long Island City, NY 11101
(718) 937-2741

SPECIALTY TRADES AND SERVICES

**Didier Chevalier
American Art Glass**
5025 Santa Monica Boulevard
Los Angeles, CA 90029
(213) 660-3359
*Specialty mirror and glass
designs*

**Ron Locks
Closet Concepts By Ron**
18812-1 Bryant Street
Northridge, CA 91324
(818) 701-6105
*Custom-lining and partition
fabrication for drawers and
inserts*

**Jim Nahigian
Plastic Mart**
(see Specialty Products)

SUGGESTED READING

Armpriester, Kate, and Mary Jane Favorite. *50 Storage Projects for the Home.* New York: Popular Science, Sterling Publishing Co., 1989.

Coen, Patricia, and Bryan Milford. *Closets: Designing and Organizing the Personalized Closet.* New York: Weidenfeld & Nicolson, 1988.

Conran, Terence. *The Kitchen Book.* New York: Crown Publishers, 1977.

Conran, Terence. *Original Designs for Kitchens and Dining Rooms.* New York: Simon & Schuster, 1990.

Conran, Terence. *The Bathroom Book.* New York: Crown Publishers, 1978.

Culp, Stephanie. *How to Conquer Clutter.* Cincinnati: Writer's Digest Books, 1989.

Culp, Stephanie. *How to Get Organized When You Don't Have the Time.* Cincinnati: Writer's Digest Books, 1986.

Culp, Stephanie. *Organized Closets and Storage: Ideas for Every Room in Your House.* Cincinnati: Writer's Digest Books, 1990.

Evatt, Crislynne. *How to Organize Your Closet... and Your Life!* New York: Balantine Books, 1980.

Frank, Beth. *Storage: Great Ideas for Closets, Kitchens, Kids' Rooms, Bathrooms, and Every Room in the House.* Los Angeles: HP Books, 1988.

Goldbeck, David. *The Smart Kitchen.* Woodstock, NY: Ceres Press, 1989.

Mack, Lorrie. *Conran's Living in Small Spaces.* Boston: Little, Brown and Company, 1988.

Mazzurco, Philip. *Media Design: Ideas and Projects for Audio, Video, and Computer Components for the Home and Office.* New York: Macmillan Publishing, 1984.

Niles, Bo, and Juta Ristsoo. *Planning the Perfect Kitchen.* New York: Simon and Schuster, 1988.

Philbin, Tom. *Cabinets, Bookcases and Closets—Basic Techniques Plus 32 Projects.* New Jersey: Creative Homeowner Press, 1980.

Schlenger, Sunny, and Roberta Roesch. *How to Be Organized in Spite of Yourself: Time and Space Management That Works With Your Personal Style.* New York: Penguin Group, 1990.

Silver, Susan. *Organized to Be the Best: Winning Solutions to Simplify How You Work.* Los Angeles: Adams Hall Publishing, 1989.

Sunset Books. *Home Offices and Workspaces.* Menlo Park, CA: Lane Publishing Co., 1986.

Sunset Books. *Planning & Remodeling Kitchens.* Menlo Park, CA: Lane Publishing Co., 1979.

Sunset Books. *Kitchens & Bathrooms Planning and Remodeling.* Menlo Park, CA: Lane Publishing Co., 1988.

Sunset Books. *Bedrooms & Bathroom Storage.* Menlo Park, CA: Lane Publishing Co., 1988.

Sunset Books. *Complete Home Storage.* Menlo Park, CA: Lane Publishing Co., 1989.

Wilkie, Jack, and Chris. *Trash and Treasure: The Complete Book About Garage Sales.* Tustin, CA: Bent Twig, 1988.

Winston, Stephanie. *Getting Organized: The Easy Way to Put Your Life in Order.* New York: W. W. Norton & Co., 1978.

Yager, Jan, Ph.D. *Making Your Office Work for You.* New York: Doubleday, 1989.

INDEX

A

Activity centers, *44, 47*
Armoires, 28, 64, 83, *153*
Art supplies, 163, *163,* 164,
  164, 165, 166
Attics, 135, 136, 137

B

Banquettes, 49
Basements, 137, 138, 139
Bathroom(s), 69–77
  children's, 71, 74
  configurations, *72, 73, 73,*
    74, 74, 75
  islands, 74
  peninsulas, 74
Bedrooms, 79–83
  children's, 80
Bookcases, 26, 136, *137*
  custom, 62
  dividing-wall, *27,* 64
  freestanding, 24
  hallway, 131
  ladders for, *33*
  recessed, *18*
Buffets, 59

C

Cabinets, 22
  bathroom, *76*
  corner, 119
  dining room, *58,* 59
  doorway, *32*
  glass-front, *44*
  kitchen, 23, *23*
  media, *17, 22, 61, 63, 67,*
    67, 82
  medicine, 75

open-front, 34
overhead, 119
pull-out, 34
recessed, *34*
shallow, *40*
wall, 66
Carts
  microwave, 51
  under-counter, *26*
Chests, *9,* 66
Children's rooms
  bathrooms, 71, 74
  bedrooms, 80
  closets in, 35
  collection displays in, 172,
    173
  hobby supply storage, 163,
    163, 164, *164, 165, 166*
Closet(s) in, *8, 11,* 85–113
  broom, 35
  cedar, 24, 41
  children's, 35, 110–113, *111*
  double-hanging, 90, *90,* 94,
    100, 104
  hangers, *100,* 101
  islands, 90, *104*
  jackets, 103
  linen, 153, *154, 154, 155, 155*
  men's, 91–98
  peninsulas, 90
  portable, 24, *151*
  shelves, *19*
  sweaters, 104
  triple-hanging in, 112
  utility, 119
  walk-in, *88,* 89, *92, 102*
  wall, 87, *88*
  women's, 99–109
Clutter, 15, 16, 17

D

Desks, 24, 28, *122,* 127, *128*
Dining rooms, 56–59
  offices in, 56, *58*
Display
  cases, *172, 173*
  racks, 24
  shelves, 131
Doors
  center-opening, 39
  pocket, 39
  retracting, 34
Drawers, 22, 26
  beverage, *52*
  organizers in, *105*
Dressing rooms, *70*

E

Efficiency, 10

F

Family rooms, 65–67
Furniture, 28, 59
  bedroom, 81, 82, 83
  dining room, 59
  knockdown, 24
  modular, 129
  office, 129

G

Garage sales, 18
Garages, 141–145, *142, 143, 144*
  expansion, 143–144
Garden sheds, 144, 145, *145*
Garment bags, *149,* 151
Glides, 38, 40
Grids, 27

H

Hallways, 38, 131, *131, 132*
Hangers, 103, 107
Hardware, 26, 27

I

Inventory, 31–35, 97–98,
  108–109
Ironing center, *119*
Islands, 35
  bathroom, 74
  closet, 90, *104*
  kitchen, 38, 44, 47, *47,* 48,
    48, 49, 51, 53, *176*

J

Jewelry storage, 167

K

Kitchen(s), *10,* 45–56
  activities, 50–53
  cabinets, 23, *23,* 44, 45
  configurations, 47, 53
  islands, 38, 44, 47, *47,* 48,
    48, 49, 51, 53, *176*
  lighting, 49
  pass-throughs, 46, 59
  peninsulas, 38, 47, *47,* 48,
    49, 50, 53

L

Landings, 38
Laundry rooms, 115–120, *116,*
  117, 118

Lighting, 24
    accent, *173*
    in basement, 137
    closet, 89
    door-activated, *55*
    in kitchen, 49
    soffit, *57*
Linens, 153, *153*, 154, *154*, 155, *155*
Living rooms, 61–64

M
Materials, 22, 41
Mobility, 24
Mudrooms, 117, 121
Murphy bed, *37*

N
Nightstands, *9*, 82

O
Office(s), 123–129, *125*, *126*
    full-time, 125
    part-time, 126
    potential locations for, *124*, 135
    space, *58*
Organization components, 9

P
Palettes
    pull-out, *83*, *95*, *99*, 129
    sliding, 26
Pantries, 45, 55, *55*, 56, *56*
Pantry, *10*, *26*, 35
Pegboard, 142, *145*
Peninsulas, 35
    bathroom, 74
    closet, 90
    kitchen, 38, *47*, *47*, 48, 49, *50*, 53
Photographs, 161, 162
Plate rails, *52*, 59, *170*
Powder rooms, 77
Purging, 15, 16, 17, 18, 141

R
Reconfiguration, 21, 23
Recycling, 18, 47, *47*
Retrievability, 22, 65, 80
Retrofitting, 37, 38, 39, 40, 41, 51

S
Safety factors for children, 50
Safes, 167, 168, *168*
Sewing equipment, 179, *179*, *180*, 181, *181*
Shelves
    adjustable, *48*, 56, *67*, 87
    book, *57*
    closet, *19*
    diagonal, *74*
    display, 131
    fixed, *40*
    garage, 142
    half, 33
    hanging, *136*
    industrial, 24
    linen, 154, 155
    open, *178*
    repositioning, 27
    risers, 33
    shallow, 34, *83*, 129, *132*
    for shoes, *21*
    stationary, 27, *27*
    track-mounted, 51
    under-cabinet, 120
    wall-mounted, 34
Sideboards, 59
Skirts, 104
Skyscraping, 49
Space evaluation, 31, 32, 33
Sports equipment, 157, *157*, 158, *158*, *159*, 160
Stairways, 35, *35*, 38
Storage, 9
    access units, 26
    active, 19
    adjustable, 21, 22
    of art supplies, 163, *163*, *164*, *164*, 165, *166*
    attic, 135, 136, 137
    audio/visual equipment, *17*, *22*, *61*, *63*, 66, 67, *67*, 82
    basements, 137, 138, 139
    bathroom, 69–77
    bedroom, 79-83
    bench, 59, *59*
    built-in, *11*, 22, *22*
    children's, 163, *163*, 164, *164*, 165, *166*. *See also* Closets, children's.
    closed, 22, *22*, 137, *140*
    clothing, 149–151. *See also* Closets.
    collections, 171, *171*, 172, *172*, 173, *173*
    contemporary, 23
    corner, 62

    custom, *16*, 23, 59
    of dresses, 105
    existing, 31, 32, 33, 34, 35
    family room, 65–67
    freestanding, 22, *22*, 24, 51, 127, *140*
    garage, 141–145
    of handbags, 107
    of hats, *99*, 103
    inactive, 19
    item-specific, 24, 25, 27, *157*
    kitchen, 45–56
    laundry room, 115–120
    linen, *68*, 153, *153*, 154, *154*, 155, *155*
    living room, 61–64
    modular, 24, *39*
    office, 123–129
    open, 23, 26, *65*, *140*
    of photographs, 161, 162
    potential, 11
    pull-out, 23, 24, 26, *48*
    retail items, 28
    rolling, 24, *139*
    seasonal, 149, *149*, 150, *150*, 151, *151*
    of sewing equipment, 179, *179*, *180*, 181, *181*
    in sheds, 149, *149*, 150, *150*, 151, *151*
    of shoes, *21*, 95, *99*, 106
    of slacks, 104
    special, 31
    of sporting equipment, 157, *157*, 158, *158*, *159*, 160
    stationary, 27
    of sweaters, 95
    of ties, 96
    traditional, 28
    types of, 21–29
    under-cabinet, 34, 51
    under-stair, 137, *138*
    valuables, 167, *167*, 168, *168*, 169
    wall-mounted, *140*
    of wine, 175, *175*, 176, *176*, *177*

T
Tables, *11*
    coffee, 24, 29, 62, 64, 66
    end, 24, 62, 66
Trays, 26, *87*, 104

V
Valuables, 167, *167*, 168, *168*, 169
Vitrines, *170*, 172

W
Wall units, 24, 25, 62
    modular, 24, 66, 67
Walls
    shelf mounting on, 34
    storage potential of, 34, 62
Window(s)
    alcoves, *81*
    seats, 33, 83
    storage under, 33, 59, 62, 64
Wine
    cellars, 176
    storage, 175, *175*, 176, *176*, *177*

ABOUT THE AUTHORS

In business since 1975, Maxine Ordesky currently operates her own space design company, Organized Designs by Maxine. Her clients include Hollywood personalities, sports figures, and high-powered professionals throughout the United States and Canada; her original organized designs have appeared several times in *Redbook* and are featured in the book *Closets*. The founding president of the National Association of Professional Organizers, Maxine lectures extensively on space planning and has been interviewed by the *L.A. Times, House & Garden, McCall's, Self, Success, Home,* and *Los Angeles* magazine in connection with her space-planning service.

Jessica Elin Hirschman, a freelance writer based in Sherman Oaks, California, is currently working on a series of design books to be published by Little, Brown in 1993. A former editor at both *Home* and *Progressive Architecture* magazines, Jessica also writes on assignments for several U.S. and foreign publications.